The

LITTLE BLACK BOOK

~ *for* ~

ENTREPRENEURS

AND THOSE WHO WANT TO BE

PETE GEISSLER

Competitive Supremacy™, Customer Collaboration™, and Intelliniche™ are trademarks of Pete Geissler and The Expressive Press.

Copyright © The Expressive Press, 2017. All rights reserved. No part of this book may be reproduced or transmitted in any form or by any means, electronic or mechanical, including photocopying, recording, or by any information storage and retrieval system, without permission in writing from the publisher.

ISBN: 9781793054586

Other Books by Pete Geissler
The Power Series:
- The Power of Writing Well
- The Power of Being Articulate
- The Power of Ethics, with Bill O'Rourke
- The Power of Dignity

The Elephant Series:
- Who Murdered Topsy?
- Who Murdered Mary?
- Who Murdered Jumbo?

The Leadership Series:
- Leadership for Profitable Sustainability
- Hugging a Cloud
- The Beanstalk Jackpots

The Lifestyle Series
- BigShots' Bull*!@#
- An Accidental Life
- Divorce Can Be Such Sweet Sorrow

Other books from The Expressive Press
- The Little Black Book of Human Resources Management, by Barry Wolfe
- Peach, by Jenevieve Woods

'There's only one corner of the universe you can be certain of improving, and that's your own self.'
Aldous Huxley, the English author who gave us Brave New World.

'I've been rich, and I've been poor. Rich is better.'
Sophie Tucker, American entertainer.

'...the discipline of entrepreneurship and innovation...applies to both existing organizations and to new ventures and to business and non-business institutions, including government.'
Peter Drucker, former Professor of Social Sciences and prolific author of business books and articles.

About The Author:

Pete Geissler is a freelance writer, professor/teacher/coach, and publisher. His impressive credentials as an entrepreneur are complemented by his academic credentials: he has been Adjunct Professor of Advanced Professional/Technical Writing, Carnegie Mellon University, and Senior Lecturer in Writing, Duquesne University Graduate School of Environmental Science and Management. He has authored many self-help books, one a publisher's best-seller; three historical fiction novellas; and has ghost-written more than three million words for Fortune 500 and other firms that have been published or spoken in formal venues.

CONTENTS

FOREWORD: Happiness Is the Ultimate Goal, and you're In the Driver's Seat 12

PROLOGUE: Who Will Benefit From This Book, and Why 14

DRIVER 1: Know and Live Your Purposes, For They Are Your Guidelines
Knowing your life's purpose(s) prevents you from irrelevant, irritating, and costly excursions that tend to hinder reaching your goals 18

DRIVER 2: Aim For Competitive Sepremacy™, For It Puts You In Charge Of Your Destiny
Competitive advantage is no longer enough; it needs muscle, insight, and more 25

DRIVER 3: Live Your Big 4 Behaviors, For They Are Your Persona
Empathize, appreciate, articulate, connect have

contributed to whatever competitive supremacy I have.
They're yours for the taking.. 32

DRIVER 4: Collaborate With Your Customers, For It Is the Ultimate Win-Win
Just as competitive advantage is too benign, customer satisfaction—and its cousin, customer delight—falls short of what's needed to meet or exceed lofty goals................. 42

DRIVER 5. Nurture And Value Your Talents And Principles, For They Are Your Conscience
Enjoying work and being overpaid are virtues that can be nurtured.. 49

DRIVER 6: Adopt These Four Rules For Creating Wealth, For They Are Your Friends
Work with a new sense of your smarts, enjoy work without guilt, exploit your education and innate intelligence, and hone your critical and creative thinking........................... 59

DRIVER 7: Create Your Own Cozy Conglomerate, For It Is Your Stability
I built my three-pronged conglomerate around words. Straying has been costly.. 69

DRIVER 8: Avoid Greed At All Costs, For Greed Is Self-Defeating
Be aware of your capacity: Overbooking and insourcing—accepting work that is beyond your capacity

to deliver a quality product on time, is one sure way to go out of business 74

DRIVER 9: Be Creative When Planning Your Future, For It Is Your Roadmap
That timeworn aphorism—if you don't plan, you plan to fail—is true for firms of any size or SIC code 81

DRIVER 10: Retain Financial Advisers You Can Trust, For They Are Your Security
Your trusted accountant and investment adviser are major keys to your success. The team's primary goal is to free your time to do more of what you do best 90

DRIVER 11: Nurture Your Most Important Asset: Your Mind and Body, for They are Your Critical Foundations
A vacation away from the rat race costs entrepreneurs twice or more than it costs employees. Is it worth it? Maybe 97

DRIVER 12: Select The Vehicle You'll Ride Into Entrepreneurship, For It Will Influence Your Wealth and Happiness
Are you an employee, intrepreneur, or entrepreneur 104

EPILOGUE: You're In the Driver's Seat 108

PETE'S PUNDITRY: Words To Play By 113

FURTHER READING

ON MONEY.. 115
ON WORK.. 116
ON COMMUNICATIONS AND THINKING........... 119

APPENDIX A. The Root Cause Of Success: Humility. 123

APPENDIX B. The Root Cause of Failure: Arrogance. 125

APPENDIX C: Your Intelniche Is Your Brand And Your Competitive Supremacy.. 128

INDEX.. 132

FOREWORD: Happiness Is the Ultimate Goal, and you're In the Driver's Seat

The happiest people I know are entrepreneurs. One, a practicing psychotherapist and professor for almost fifty years, admits to an annual income below $90K and to a portfolio below $800K. She finds her patients 'fascinating' and her students 'engrossing', and is dedicated to improving their lives. She has said to me on several occasions, 'I change lives for the better by changing thinking and behavior, just as you do.' She has developed her intelliniche in addiction therapy, and she constantly improves her skills and mind by attending conferences throughout North America, then, after reading the books she invariably brings home, she places them in her waiting room for patients to borrow and read.

Another is the founder and CEO of a small engineering firm with 15 employees. He founded his firm after being disillusioned by the shortsighted leaders of the huge firm where he toiled as manager of a design team, figuring he could do better. He has developed such a strong intelliniche that he is an oligopoly, bordering on monopoly. He sharpens his skills by contributing articles to a national trade magazine, writing a textbook that he thinks will soon set the standard for his profession, and teaching an on-line course. He lives large in modest homes in Pittsburgh and South Carolina, playing golf, and collecting muscle cars. He estimates his income as 'around $100K' and his liquid assets as well below $300k.

My third example is a woman of 76 years who is a one-person accounting firm for several small businesses. She has never earned more than $50k a year—'enough for me to live comfortably'—owns a small condo in an upscale suburban town, and is perhaps the strongest advocate I know of self-reliance and Generous Free Enterprise. Her liquid assets are below $250K, and she carries no debt, not even a mortgage or car payment. Her personal balance sheet is all assets and no liabilities, and her operating statement includes 20 percent of her income in escrow for emergencies.

All live the 12 Drivers.

PROLOGUE: Who Will Benefit From This Book, and Why

I wrote this book to share my lessons learned—my 12 drivers—as I, an ordinary person with ordinary talents and smarts, journeyed to an extraordinary life of extreme happiness. I am your template; any sentient, curious, and ambitious person can emulate my journey at any time.

Readers who will benefit from living this book's habits are willing and able to accept that:

1. **Success transcends wealth, fame, and power, and extends into happiness, fulfillment, meaning, and legacy.** Everybody has their personal definition of success, and it typically revolves about wealth, fame, and power. My former publisher, for example, defines success as being rich enough to be happy. Those who subscribe to that simplistic and fallacious definition are missing a personal calling to create meaning—whatever matters to you—and to make a positive difference in the lives of others.

2. **Security lies in self-reliance, which probably means being an intrapreneur or entrepreneur.** The vast majority—I've read up to 80 percent—of new jobs is created by small business. In my experience, large companies and their employees come and go at the whim of mismanagement. Two examples that hurt me and thousands of others are Westinghouse and Dravo, two century-old companies with laudable reputations for paternalistic personnel policies. There are many others extending as far back as ENRON's bankruptcy in the 1990s that hurt thousands of employees who thought that they had jobs for life or years. In essence, the only difference between working for yourself and working for others is control over your future.

3. **The 12 drivers are from a practitioner with modest academic credentials.** I have more than 25 books in my small library that claim to tell me how to succeed in business; professors of business who ply their trade at prestigious universities authored all but two. They posit useful theories and then support them with data from annual reports and interviews with top execs ... second- and third-hand knowledge. On the other hand, this book was written by a seasoned practitioner who never rose above adjunct professor and senior lecturer at two universities. Every word in the book is based on first-hand experience and empirical knowledge.

This book is a retrospective on a life that I was privileged to have lived for more than half a century. Its drivers are proven to be, above all, immediately applicable and realistic. Readers are not burdened by theories that have not been tested for years in the battles that are constantly being fought in the real worlds of commerce.

This book is not for people who think that the road to success is to hit the lottery or becoming the close relative of a rich uncle. It is for people who aspire to a life of quiet affluence and happiness, which I think is possible for millions of people who align their expectations with reality.

I am not particularly bright, prophetic, or insightful. According to my clients and friends, I am particularly intuitive and dedicated to my craft. Some say that I was fortunate, and I agree that some good fortune, aka luck, played its part. A favorite author and business guru, Peter Drucker, said that, 'I was lucky. When God rained manna from heaven, I had a spoon.' He didn't know that while he was referring to himself he was also referring to me, and, I hope, you. I want to amend his words ever so slightly: When the deity of choice was raining sustenance from heaven, I was caught in the downpour and was ready for a picnic with beer, mustard, utensils, and ant repellent. You can join me.

I succeed by being a symbiotic, one-person conglomerate based on words—I often call it my 'cozy conglomerate' it is so tightly laced. I'm a professional/technical writer, a teacher/professor of professional/technical writing, and an author/publisher of self-help books, many of them based on the importance of writing well. The three legs of my conglomerate are infamous for creating more poverty than wealth. Nevertheless, they have served me well, perhaps because I love what I do, I love the people I do it with, and I love how it shows in my smile and optimism.

I am happier than I ever thought was possible, which makes me thankful all over again. In those senses, my many friends tell me that I am a rare bird—so rare that I should tell the world how it all happened and those in the world who are so inclined can follow my lead.

— Pete Geissler

PS: If you haven't done it already, perhaps now is the time to redefine success to align with your expectations and encompass more than wealth. The drivers in this book, which are my contract with you, will help. I validate them with front-line experiences that you can emulate if you are motivated to do so. As you redefine, remember that every person holds in their mind a definition of success and that every person's path to it is difficult, circuitous, and exclusively theirs. I am your guide, not your overseer.

DRIVER 1: Know and Live Your Purposes, For They Are Your Guidelines

Knowing your life's purpose(s) keeps you on the track that you've decided is best for you. It shapes your decisions and prevents you from irrelevant, irritating, and costly excursions that tend to hinder reaching your goals.

Peter Drucker said that the sovereign purpose of an enterprise is profitability. Herbert Hoover disagreed when he said that American business needs a purpose greater than the struggle of materialism. I think that those thoughts apply to individuals as well, especially entrepreneurs like me, as do the three authors of *Success Built to Last*. They posit that making money, making a difference, and living a life with meaning are compatible goals, with meaning the more important. I agree, and nobody would ever dub me a starry-eyed idealist.

I formed my first company, Geissler Inc., strictly and solely to write for the many Fortune 500 firms in Pittsburgh at the time that needed to communicate better and could pay my fees. You could say that I was in it for the money, and you'd be spot on, almost. I also went into business because I love to play with words. In fact, I tumbled madly in love with words when I was a teen ager and fell into the spell of marvelous teacher whose love for words was both palpable and infectious.

I remember clearly, some twenty years after high school when I received my first check for my writing, and I shouted my joyous epiphany to a friend: 'You mean I can be paid for doing what I love? Wow!'

I became a writer long before I became a business. I loved the image, the cachet, of being a writer, the image of being offbeat, unconventional, a bit drunk, and a free and disheveled spirit. I loved, and still love being asked at various social events what I do for a living and saying with obvious glee, 'I'm a writer' and watching their eyes widen and then reply, 'I always wanted to write', implying that they have always wanted to be me. Pretty heady stuff, being a role model even in my small circle.

But the real, best, and most important reason for being an entrepreneur is freedom, a squishy and huge concept that takes on many meanings. First, it means that I alone control my present and future happiness and security. I can do that because I can pick my bosses, aka my clients, and embrace those I like and pay my fees—note the two criteria—and discard those that I don't like and can't or won't pay. That's impossible if you work for a larger organization in which some invisible hand from on high picks your proximate boss, as well as your bosses on the many rungs of the corporate ladder above you.

Freedom extends to lifestyle, which in my case is a mixed bag. Surely, one of the many joys in being an entrepreneur is being able to work or not work on my own schedule. I love logging billable hours whenever I want, which often is in the very early morning or the middle of the night or during a holiday such as Christmas - whenever the urge hits or I get an idea/inspiration that can't wait until 'normal working hours', which means nada to me. I can grab a beer, martini, or coffee and log billable hours on the patio behind my house. I can dress in leisure pants and a tee shirt in my office and change quickly, ala Clark Kent in a phone booth—how's that for a tired vision? —into one of my several designer suits and run off to a top level meeting in an ivory corporate tower, and nobody is the wiser.

A friend told me that he could not live such a double life. He does not understand that I am the same person regardless of my clothes, and that playing the corporate game is one way to financial freedom, the one I had chosen. Back in the roaring 1920s a naive reporter supposedly asked Willy Sutton, the famous bank robber, 'Why do you rob banks?' Willy replied, 'Because that's where the money is.' Why do I work for billion-dollar corporations?

In short, I enjoy being thought of as a touch eccentric. My Mother didn't. She died convinced that I was living in a windy, unheated garret dressed in rags, cooking beans on a hot plate, and sopping up the booze ala Hemingway and Fitzgerald and Faulkner. I can only wish that she was right and I was playing with those famous writers.

My Evolving Purposes:

I believe that life is a constantly changing series of goals and circumstances to which every sentient person must adjust and which make life worth the tremendous effort—the sacrifice and dedication—many of us expend willingly to make it all worthwhile, to make it joyous, comfortable, and fulfilled.

Therefore, **everyone needs a statement of purpose that adjusts in lockstep with changes in life,** just as every business needs statements of its vision and mission that change as the business evolves. My purposes morphed in three stages as I and my business morphed from a freelance writer into the cozy conglomerate and I from a responsible father and husband to a single grandparent. I might say that I morphed from making a living to making a life, which is now termed a balanced life, i.e. one that considers the needs for cash and the needs for social satisfaction. *My purposes:*

1. **Wealth:** To earn money by exploiting my abilities with words and my natural intelligence and curiosity—aka

my imagination—all the while nurturing my love for an artistic lifestyle that allows me to be a free spirit.

I was working as a sales engineer for a small construction company—just months before I saw the light and became a 'reformed engineer' and then a writer—when the CEO got an itch to advertise, appointed me Ad Manager, and told me to work with a friend from Yale who owned a small agency. The CEO tasked us initially to create a brochure and other marketing pieces. I knew little about the process and welcomed the opportunity. One day we were walking to lunch and he asked if I would write the text for a brochure for one of his tech clients; neither he nor the writers on his staff knew the subject well enough to write about it intelligently. I wrote the text, and he was pleased enough to pay me a small fee and shower me with additional work, initiating my career as a professional writer.

2. **Wealth, prestige, and conscience:** To teach others to write and help them reap the benefits of good writing, just as I have, my idea of paying back society for my good fortune.

I was helping my soos—significant other, opposite sex—to write a long memo to her boss when she stopped and said, 'You should teach. You've helped me to be a better writer and I'm sure that you can help others.'

I called the English Department at the University of Pittsburgh and, after a short meeting, the chair hired me to teach an introductory course in writing as an adjunct professor. One of my first students, an engineer, worked with my soos and was about to lose his job because he could not express himself in writing. He told me a year later that my instruction saved his job and career, an ego builder for a fledgling teacher. Encouraged, I went on to teach Advanced Writing at Carnegie Mellon University, then at The Graduate School of Environmental Science and Management, Duquesne University, and now at various engineering and environmental consulting firms.

A Costly Misstep: I fed my conscience by joining the boards of four non-profits, all involved in the performing arts or literature. All initially were eager to tap into my skills as a writer and manager. I soon found that they were interested only in my donations and my rubber-stamp approval of the status quo, to not rock the boat I resigned from all, disillusioned, my conscience intact but bruised.

3. **Wealth, prestige, conscience, and legacy:** My third and continuing phase of my purposeful life is to add my legacy to wealth, prestige, and conscience.

I think of my legacy as, first, my four children and six grandchildren, then my hundreds of students who I hope I have helped live a more fulfilled life, and last my books. To that end, I continue to teach at consulting firms and to write and publish books such as this one. I transferred the rights to my writing seminars to a former student at Duquesne University, and transferred ownership of my publishing company and its books to my three associates. I also have formed a mythical 'Fan Club' comprised of my former students, and appointed a president who credits me with her success as a Senior Environmental Scientist with a global consulting firm.

* *

If life were simple, we could all sail through it with unchanging purpose(s), but it isn't and we can't if we want to be happy. Pity the persons who live without purpose, for their lives are directionless and futile and they are frustrated and complaining. Do not join them.

DRIVER 2: Aim For Competitive Sepremacy™, For It Puts You In Charge Of Your Destiny

Competitive advantage is no longer enough; it is far too benign, too docile, too narrow, too just plain lazy and common. The idea is just fine; it just needs to be more broad and aggressive. It needs to be redefined, repurposed, and restated.

Enter Competitive Supremacy™. It espouses all three elements of competitive advantage—the leverage that a business of any size or type has over its competitors—plus a fourth element, a set of behaviors that is forgotten by too many of our business schools and companies: to empathize, appreciate, articulate, and connect. Some of my clients call that foursome of behaviors 'common courtesy', and wish for more of it in the world. I do too. I call it 'the awesome power of dignity' or of decency, or of respect, and wish more people would exploit it.

Perhaps this book will help.

Conventional businesspersons and professors who have never managed a business typically define competitive advantage by three elements:

1. Cost leadership is a business' ability to produce a product or service at a lower cost than competitors' cost without compromising quality or schedule. If the business is able to produce the same quality product, deliver it on time, and sell it for less, it enjoys a competitive advantage.

Or does it. Cost is only one part of value, and in my case, it surely is not the most important. One of my clients said to me often that I was his only supplier for whom he could not assign an hourly rate, and he didn't care: He was happy with 'the no-hassle job' that I supplied, and the satisfaction of his bosses with the results of my work.

I was fortunate to work for clients who respected my talents enough to be less concerned with price—their cost—and more concerned with value, a squishy term that each of us defines in our own head. I have often said that the most expensive communications—a website, speech, marketing plan etc. —is the one that doesn't do its job, even if it cost a mere dollar. The same is true of any product.

I was talking to a small group of business owners and one related how he had written an article about his company for a trade magazine and it was rejected by the editor as 'poorly conceived and worded'. He bragged that 'it didn't cost a dime'. 'Not so', I replied. 'It cost you the hours and anguish you spent writing a piece of no value, so your cost was infinite. If you don't think so, then you do not value your time or talent'.

I then offered to write his article for $3000 and guarantee placement in the same magazine, and he and others in the group laughed. I stopped their fun by asking: 'Tell me; which article is more expensive, his of no value or mine of the value he wanted.' Silence.

2. Differential advantage was once called 'positioning' and is more recently called 'branding' or 'niche marketing'. Regardless of its tag, when a business' products or services are different, supposedly better than its competitors', consumers are willing to pay more for the difference, regardless of whether they perceive the difference to be real or bogus.

I was lunching with colleagues at Carnegie Mellon University when one asked me if I was busily writing for business and how much I charged. 'I'm busier than ever, and I have an hourly rate in my head but never tell clients unless they insist or I'm working for a government agency, which is rare. I think that hourly rates are the dumbest way to charge for an esoteric service like mine, and I should charge for my value, which often exceeds my rates by a considerable margin.'

'Isn't that unethical?'

'No, It's good business, and in thirty years only one of my clients complained. I often say, without a bit of evidence to back me up, that I am the busiest and most expensive writer in town, and if a client does not recognize that as value, he or she is too naive to play in my sandbox.'

3. Focus advantage—also called segmentation advantage—aims marketing at a few target markets rather than all or everyone, and, according to a Harvard professor, is essential for small businesses without the resources for broad-based marketing. Bull. Every business of every size and type focuses its marketing on a target market or two. An easy example: Rolls Royce and Rolex do not waste resources on selling me overpriced (you now know why I don't own either) cars and watches; my net worth might qualify me, barely, to be a buyer, but my buying habits and the neighborhood in which I live do not by a long shot.

My financial adviser—most of us need one—and I suggest that retaining one early in your lucrative career will pay off big down the road—is the perfect template. One of his mantras is 'we're not for everyone.' He segments his market to include only investors with the patience to stay the course during financial downturns despite the temptation to sell. He eschews fear and greed.

I too am not for everyone. I am fond of saying that I know how to market nuclear plants worth billions of dollars to a hand full of buyers, perhaps the tightest of niche markets.

But I cannot market paper clips worth less than a penny that are marketed to billions of buyers, perhaps the closest market to that elusive 'everyone' or 'general'. And I can teach engineers and scientists how to write proposals and reports, but not the house wife or purchasing agent or retail clerk who want to write the Great American Novel, so I don't try.

I know a consulting company whose goal is to be so supreme, so amazingly aggressive, that its CEO urges its thousands of employees to be so valuable to clients that they drive all competitors out of business, and he does mean all. Of course, he and his employees know that the goal is unrealistic, but that doesn't stop them from trying vainly to meet it. Must be frustrating.

I, on the other hand, think that they are terribly misguided. I love my good competitors and hope that they stay in business. I have even helped them stay in business. A respected writer, for example, asked me to help write a speech on a technical topic that he did not grasp. I did, he converted my writing style to his—was that plagiarism? — and the speech was a hit with his client and his client's audience. He turned his fee over to me, and we both won, he by retaining a client, and me by banking a fee that I did not expect.

My reasons for loving my good competitors are strictly selfish: good competitors (please note the emphasis on good, aka competent and respected) encourage and enlarge the market for all, while bad competitors shrink it. Nothing enlarges the market more than an experience that exceeds expectations. When that happens, the client becomes repeat business and the evangelist, the advocate or ambassador, for the service if not the specific supplier, and that helps suppliers and clients. On the other hand, nothing sours a client more quickly than an experience that falls short of expectations.

Two recent experiences: A friend and entrepreneur retained a financial adviser who turned out to be an incompetent charlatan. My friend fired his adviser and refuses to retain another despite recommendations to do so. He now manages his own assets, shrinking his productivity, billable hours, and the market for advisers as he tells others of his disillusionment. I purchased a new Ford with a dangerously defective transmission and lost more than $25,000 when I traded for a car that I could trust. I won't buy another Ford ever again, and neither, I hope, will the dozens of potential buyers to whom I told this sordid tale, including you. Ford is too big to care, but I do.

* *

Your good competitors are your friends and can be your customers that you encourage to stay in business; your bad competitors are your enemies that you can encourage to go out of business. No matter how strong your competitive position, it will disappear if you can't support it with the appropriate behaviors for an extended period of time, which brings me to...

DRIVER 3: Live Your Big 4 Behaviors, For They Are Your Persona

Empathize, appreciate, articulate, and connect have been my constant companions and guidelines throughout my 50+ years in business, and I am certain that they have contributed to whatever competitive supremacy I have.

Please note that I've expressed the Big 4 Behaviors as action verbs, not the lazy nouns empathy, appreciation, articulation, and connection. Note also that the behaviors are rare, at least in my circle, and I assume in others. Note also that the four are inseparable and synergistic, and that they are yours for the taking and for a lifetime.

To Empathize is to continuously read the mind of another person to discover their point of view and experience; it is to be sensitive to another person's needs, wants, fears and concerns. It is accurate when it is based on objective evaluations of reality, not guesses. It is not sympathy, which is subjective, typically based on emotions such as pity or sorrow.

A friend and satellite client visited my home office regularly to enjoy a free cocktail and to gossip. As his drinking evolved to the point where he was staggering and slurring, I became so concerned about his driving that I called my lawyer to determine my liability should he be tagged for a DUI or be in an accident. I became so angry with his drinking that I said to him and others that I didn't care if he killed himself in an accident—heartless of me, eh?—but I would feel very guilty if he killed someone else.

My lawyer gave me some advice that I have never forgotten, 'You may or may not be liable for his behavior, the law is unclear, but regardless—why do you want to associate with a toxic freeloader?'

I asked my toxic freeloader and a neutral friend to meet me at a nearby bar instead of my home, freeing me from even a hint of liability by transferring it to the bar owner. I expressed my concerns and, in the perfect example of denial and lack of empathy, he shouted 'bullshit' three times. I told him that he was not welcome in my home and he told me not to worry, he wouldn't cross my threshold. I left happier and relieved, and I hope that he did too. BTW, my neutral friend agreed with me and still visits regularly.

A client and I were discussing his upcoming speech when he told me that my most important service to him was not my memorable prose. Instead, my greater value was my penchant for asking 'Do you really want to say that to this audience?', I knew then at some mindful level that I was empathizing with him by asking him to empathize with his publics. In short, I was asking him to be a successful presenter. We both knew that a speech that failed to relate to the needs and wants of his audience would fall flat, be ignored, and fail to deliver the message.

Empathy enters into most—dare I say 'every?' —facet of our lives, from sales and leadership to management and communications to romance, parenting, advertising, and political action. The failure to empathize manifests itself at its most traumatic in psychopaths, rapists, criminals, and on a less dramatic level in lost sales and elections, vague leadership, and divorce.

An example: I was attending a conference on cleaning sulfurous gasses emitted from coal-fired power plants. My task was to report later what I learned from a series of speeches by experts in the field. The audience was some 80 chemical engineers or managers eager to learn how to comply with environmental regulations at the lowest possible cost.

A manufacturer of the pumps critical to plant operations lost his way. Instead of addressing the concerns of the audience—operating issues such as the pumps' efficiency, reliability, and extended warranty and maintenance schedule—the presenter addressed the wonders of design and metallurgy.

The audience didn't care and soon started to fidget and discuss among themselves the upcoming lunch and golf tournament, quite rudely but proof positive that audiences can be cruel when you waste their time. The presenter was soon talking to himself, his message was not delivered, and he lost the considerable costs of travel to the conference and productive time at his offices. He might have lost sales.

When I asked him later what he thought went wrong, he said quite correctly that he had misjudged his audience, had lost his connection by assuming that they would be interested in what interested him. I asked if he had called the sponsors of the conference to get a handle on the audience, and he mused, 'I never thought of that'.

To Appreciate is to be grateful or thankful and express it in words and deeds. It is to esteem and recognize another person for what he or she is and means to your relationship.

I wrote many speeches for an EVP and loved collaborating with him on every one. He always, before speaking, rehearsed with me to hone his technique and to be sure that I had not written words over which he could stumble or sentences so long that he would run out of breath. Then, after speaking, he invariably called to thank me for helping him to be a 'star' (his sobriquet) and to alert me to the next assignment. I always congratulated him and reminded him that he does the same for me—makes me a star—by guiding me into the content and rehearsing. We were the perfect win-win, and our relationship extended for years.

To Articulate is to express ideas clearly and concisely. I daresay that I've written more than 50 thousand words on the connections between the ability to articulate with success in business/politics/life/and happiness. And I daresay that I've spoken more than 50 thousand words on the same subject to my classes and in all sorts of lectures to all sorts of audiences. You might say that it is one of my many passions.

A study by The Johnson O'Connor Research Institute ignited my passion. It connected vocabulary—the number of words a person knows the meaning of and can use in intelligent writing and speaking—with height on any organization chart. The connection was so compelling to me that I wrote an entire book based on it.

Then I ran into a quote by one of America's great business gurus, Peter Drucker: *'The one basic skill need for success in business is the ability to clearly express ideas in writing and speaking.'* I think that Peter's admonition is incomplete: The one basic skill for success in business **and in life is** the ability to clearly and concisely express ideas in writing and speaking.

Dennis Slevin, a friend and professor of management at the Katz Graduate School of Business, University of Pittsburgh, agrees by noting in his book *The Whole Manager* that 'Communication skills are essential for managerial success. The average manager can ask literally hundreds of questions in a typical meeting...perhaps he has learned the costs of communication breakdowns ...'

Writing and speaking are only half of being articulate; the other half is listening to yourself and to others, perhaps the ultimate empathy. Only then can you know the subject well enough to write and speak about it, and, in a broader sense, to anticipate change and adapt to it. For example, I was writing a series of speeches for several executives at a large manufacturer, and I heard hints that the company might be in trouble, along with my income. I opened doors at another company that I figured would fill in the coming income gap. It worked, and, while my income dropped a bit, I muddled through and survived.

I've been telling all sorts of folks for at least 30 years that good writing and speaking are the keys to success in no matter how it's defined.

The Wall Street Journal, in its September 2002, supplement, The Top Business Schools, finally caught the brass ring by affirming that good writing is key to promotability, productivity, and profitability, and that universities, especially technical and business schools, still ignore this simple reality.

A few pivotal points from the articles: Communications and Interpersonal Skills were ranked as desirable assets by more recruiters [90 percent] than any of the other 26 desirable attributes considered. It nosed out Ability to

Work Well within a Team (87 percent, and impossible without communications skills), and Analytical and Problem-Solving Abilities (86 percent, also impossible without vocabulary).

Yet employers say that graduates' writing is 'appalling', and it stays that way for years. 'Communications and other so-called soft skills are what corporate recruiters' (and, presumably, corporate managers) 'crave most but find most elusive in MBA and other graduates.' Many professors and administrators miss these connections: Teaching soft skills 'takes away time and money from more serious academic disciplines'.

Considering the comments in the WSJ, what more serious disciplines could they have in mind?

Communications and leadership skills are linked; entrepreneurs and corporate managers cannot lead if they cannot clearly articulate their vision and purpose. And communications skills are linked to personal growth: 'MBA and other graduates may get by on their technical and quantitative skills the first couple of years out of school. But soon, leadership and communications skills come to the fore in distinguishing the entrepreneurs and managers whose careers really take off.'

Not long ago I asked the dean of a Pittsburgh B-school and former president of a major manufacturer what his clients—hirers of his graduates—complained about most.

His reply: 'The most frequent and vehement negative criticism from customers, and others, too, about employees at all levels is that they can't communicate! They can't talk in cohesive, coherent sentences. More important, they can't write, can't express their ideas on paper. We may have trained a brilliant technical or analytical mind, but how would anyone know?'

You can read his complete comments—and the comments from many other executives and leaders—in my book: ***The Power of Being Articulate.***

Ralph Waldo Emerson said that *'It is a luxury to be understood.'* I disagree: It is a necessity to be understood for everyone who dreams of financial and social success.

To Connect is to visibly wiggle into the minds of clients as often as possible. *'Out of sight, out of mind'* will kill any business. I reverse the thought to be positive: *'in sight, in mind'* will nurture any business.

I did the usual things to be 'in mind': acknowledge birthdays and anniversaries, and attend all sorts of dinners and cocktail parties disguised as fundraisers, conventions, symposia, and just plain gatherings of people who could positively influence my life and income. I bought a designer tux and a closet full of designer suits to give the impression of mild affluence, knowing full well that my clients, many of them upper-crust, upper-income executives want to work with people who mirror themselves, another example of empathy and one of the first rules of persuasion.

I also joined a posh golf club and sponsored 'The World's Most Exclusive Invitational', to which I invited eleven of my best clients. At the after-golf dinner, I announced the winner and presented him/her with an original framed photograph of a golf ball in dewy grass that I commissioned from a prominent local photographer. Several of the winners have hung their photo in their offices and dens; they are constant reminders of how much I empathize with and appreciate them. BTW, I hung one photo on the wall of my library and I am amazed at how many people want to know the story behind it.

Probably my most productive act of connecting is my habit of showing up unannounced on random Friday evenings at a bistro in the basement of the headquarters building of my most prominent client. A dozen or so middle managers habitually met there for a bit of grog and gossip before venturing home and starting the weekend. I was always welcome to join them, perhaps because I tended to pick up the tab, but more likely (each of them could easily afford to pay) to ask my opinion of the latest moves by top management and rumors of promotions and firings. Yes, because many of the company's business units retained me and I was privy to the thinking of a broad spectrum of their execs, I was a reliable source of gossip throughout the company. I always respected confidential information and they respected my silence when it was called for.

All that aside, I never solicited work when there—the ultimate soft sell—and rarely left without paying a big bill for booze and food along with several requests to 'call me Monday; I have an assignment for you.'

My soos accompanied me on several occasions, and after one she commented, 'Do you know how much you spent?' 'Nothing, not a dime', I replied, boggling her accountant's mind. 'The cost of the evening will easily be absorbed by my fees, and they know very well it will be and don't care.'

* *

The Big 4 Behaviors are basic to a civil society and to your image as a person who treats others with the respect they deserve. It is akin to 'do unto others ... with an addendum: 'Also do unto yourself'.

DRIVER 4: Collaborate With Your Customers, For It Is the Ultimate Win-Win

Just as competitive advantage is too lazy to be a useful goal, customer satisfaction and its cousin, customer delight, sit on their lazy butts and fall short of what's needed to meet or exceed the realistically lofty goals of those who aspire to be successful entrepreneurs.

Enter Customer Collaboration™, an active and conscious process that guarantees your #1 spot in the hearts and minds of those who pay your bills, and guarantees their #1 spot in your heart and mind. It is akin to cooperation to meet shared goals that I think of as far deeper than partnership. The former EVP at Westinghouse and CEO of GenCorp, John Yasinsky, likens it to mutual alignment of strategies and tactics. I think of it as those tried and true aphorisms. 'you scratch my back and I'll scratch yours', and 'what's good or the goose is good for the gander'.

'Collaboration' has its sinister connotations, made popular in spy novels or documentaries as in 'collaborating with the enemy.' My Oxford's first definition is 'to work jointly', with synonyms 'to cooperate, work together, team up.' Its second definition is 'to cooperate traitorously as with an enemy', which of course doesn't fit the context of this book or of my or your businesses.

My concept of customer collaboration dispels any hint of an adversarial, sinister, or fraudulent relationship, or of working toward cross-purposes. Those destructive behaviors rear their ugly heads perhaps because the parties do not know or are not willing to admit that they share the same purposes. A good example might be buying a car: the seller strives for the highest price, the buyer the lowest, when each wants a fair price for both.

Divorce is another example that hits home. I wonder if spouses realize that each is striving for a peaceful settlement that allows them to move on to the next phase of their lives without scarring their children. It reminds me of that old truism that a successful negotiation satisfies—meets the expectations—of all parties. And, as long as I am on this topic, I deplore books such as *Men Are From Mars, Women Are From Venus* and its many successors. Their purpose is to sell books by creating controversy, while in truth both sexes want the same comfort, security, love and respect, to be treated kindly and with dignity. To be treated with the Big 4 Behaviors, aka decency.

In my business, and I think in every business, collaboration means that I work to make my client employee of the month, or CEO of the year, or communicator of the year, or just so amazingly happy with what I do that he or she hires me for the next job. On the other side of the coin, my clients work toward making me supplier of the year and spread the word about my value to colleagues and competitors so that I stay in business. Everybody wins.

Example: My client and I were discussing what we learned after two days of meetings about a new way to position and market a major product line that would increase market share and profits. We each had ideas—brochures, direct mail, a new website—that we discarded as 'conventional, not different, not dramatic', surely not the breakthrough that we needed.

Then he came up with a way to inspire customers to quantify the long-term value of the product versus the long-term value of similar products offered by a plethora of competitors, and The Value Factor was born. The entire marketing program included the usual brochures, plus training of the sales force in a completely new sales approach, and software to ease the evaluation process.

One result was a 3-point increase in market share and more than $100 million in profitable sales. The local advertising trade association named my client 'marketer of the year', and he named me his valuable sidekick 'couldn't have done it without Pete', he said in his acceptance speech to hundreds of his peers and my current or potential clients. The program was expanded to many other product lines, and I, the guy who ran with the idea and created the marketing communications and training course, was showered with work at my highest fees, which was only natural since I had carved out a the ultimate niche and ego booster, an intellectual monopoly. (See Driver 5 for another example of that covert unfair advantage.)

I worked so closely and often with another marketing manager with the same company that he called me his 'phantom staff'. I was in effect on his payroll, and we both benefitted with accolades and cash, his with ego-building raises and me with asset-building fees. BTW, he and his peers asked several times during my career if I would consider working on retainer, and I always refused. Sure, it would guarantee a certain income level. On the other hand, it would require me to reveal my hourly rates and to keep detailed records. I didn't like the tradeoff.

I think of my financial manager in the same way; we collaborate to make each other financially comfortable. He does that by understanding my goals—empathy again—and I do that by recommending friends who might become new clients—appreciation again. In short, we collaborate to stay in business and to thrive.

He and 80 others were at my 75th birthday bash and, as we looked at the revelers, I asked how many I had sent to him and became his clients. 'A bunch', he replied, maybe because he ran out of fingers and toes. No wonder we are friends as well as business associates.

Collaboration starts with empathizing to know, not guess, the needs and wants of customers, then proceeds to appreciating their business and friendship, then showing your appreciation in words and deeds, and finally keeping in touch without selling. I call it the velvet touch.

I learned early in my career that my customers, all employees of large firms with multiple layers of overbearing and watchful bosses, yearned to escape their offices for friendlier environs. I also learned that acceptable escapes were golf courses and suppliers' offices, both of which are traditional venues for serious business discussions, which they can be but often fall short of that ideal.

So, naturally, I showed my appreciation of their needs and wants by joining an upper-crust golf club and arranged with the manager and pro to bend the rules and allow my customers to play, eat, and drink there even if I wasn't with them. The club appreciated the extra revenue, and my clients appreciated the freedom to play, drink, and eat when they wanted. BTW, they took advantage of my generosity but never abused it with excessive expenditures—and I spread the cost over my fees without anyone noticing. (Is that unethical?) It's amazing what an extra billable hour or two can pay for.

My golf club was a big asset in many ways, but it was almost insignificant compared to my home office. My dining room became a plush conference room akin to a boardroom in which anyone could be totally comfortable for business or social gatherings. I installed a wet bar and stocked it with top-shelf booze, the exact kinds that each client preferred. Yes, I served their drugs of choice. One client remarked, 'I have never seen such an overthe-top array of expensive liquor and wine in a home, and it's free', which of course it isn't, as he knows.

My clients clamored to meet with me late afternoons, aka cocktail hour, explaining to their bosses that they had urgent business to discuss with me. We all knew that often it was bullshit; we also knew that it was fun, profitable, my route to repeat business and their route to reliable consulting... another win-win. And I knew, as did my more astute customers, that it cost me nada, just as my golf club cost nada.

A competent writer who liked to think of himself as a competitor but really never came close, noticed my modus operandi and told me that he couldn't afford it, proving that he did not understand the rudiments of accounting and marketing in our respective businesses, and he certainly did not understand the Big 4. He elected and preferred, in his naiveté, to constantly scramble for new business and endure the extreme ups and downs of his revenue stream when the constancy of repeat business is so much less expensive and within his grasp. He is at the top my list of the worst businesspersons that I have encountered.

* *

Customer Collaboration is embedded in one of my favorite aphorisms: good customers make good suppliers, and good suppliers make good customers—a kind of symbiosis that can't happen with adversarial or one-way relationships. The same is true with spouses and spouses, lovers and lovers, friends and friends.

DRIVER 5. Nurture And Value Your Talents And Principles, For They Are Your Conscience

You and I, ambitious and dedicated as we are, cannot possibly enjoy life if we have a TGIF attitude, or if we count the days to that illusion of happiness called retirement. One of my clients called retirement 'a vile condition brought about by age and befuddled management'. Your career or profession—let's drop 'work' simply because of its negative connotations held by people who haven't experienced the joys of accomplishment. Your career or profession is a reflection of your important values, which is far more than your need for money. It is, or it should and can be, your second-most important source of satisfaction and relationships (behind your family), and an outlet for your creativity. If it isn't, think about changing.

Steve Jobs is famous for admonishing the 2005 graduates of Stanford University, *'The only way to do great work is to love what you do. If you haven't found it yet, keep looking. Don't settle.'* Steve was only half right: Many businesses were started to fill a perceived or actual need. I started my publishing business, for example, because I was so dissatisfied and disillusioned, aka pissed off, with established publishers that I figured I could do better, not because I had a burning desire to take on another business challenge. Now **The Expressive Press** is the third leg of my cozy conglomerate.

I read the book, **Do What You Love, The Money Will Follow,** after I had been in business for a dozen years or so, and it confirmed in hard text what I already knew intuitively—that I would enjoy first and prosper second. The book also prompted me to ask: Is enjoying work a product of nature or nurture? You decide.

My father loved his work as a respected mechanical engineer. When he arrived at our home in suburban New York some 25 miles away by commuter train from his job in Manhattan, he kissed and said hello to his wife and kids, ate dinner, and disappeared into a basement filled with metalworking tools where he built models for the machines he invented for making the sugar in your kitchen. He died at age 93 in good health and with more than 30 patents, a modest estate, and no debts. In many ways I am his clone, especially if you can think of his patents being akin to my books, and patents and books as legacy.

When my father died, the preacher asked me what one word described his life. I replied, 'responsible'. I wish that

I could have replied 'loving', and he was in his own responsible way. I now think of being responsible as one of the more important and subtle manifestations of love. I only hope that my kids and grandkids can say the same about me.

A less active but important client—all of them are important to some degree, but the more active are the more important—phoned: 'You're the only writer in this town that can handle this project, a complicated financial analysis of one of our construction products. I could hire a writer from New York, but I'd rather not. Can you do it?' That call as my first insight into my intellectual monopoly, or oligopoly, and it helped to create my Intelleniche that I describe in APPENDIX C.

I was totally intrigued with a huge challenge that would add prestige to my portfolio and big bucks to my bank account. I wanted the work, but explained that I was committed for six months with writing a series of speeches for another client. Could this project wait?

The lesser client said he'd think about it and would call me back. He did, and he retained me for one of the largest and most interesting assignments of my career. Not only did I collect a handsome fee, I befriended my primary source of information, an offbeat architect with a leaning toward fine art and a quirky lifestyle that mirrored mine.

I could have accepted the assignment and worked many hours to complete it and the speeches, but that would demonstrate that I do not value my talents enough to ask for reasonable concessions. *And it would have violated DRIVER 8, Avoid Greed and one of its destructive signs, overbooking.*

I was complimented beyond my wildest expectations when an active client responded to this request from a colleague, 'Can you suggest a writer for this difficult assignment?' My client suggested me with these words: 'Pete Geissler; he is very good.' While I was flattered by his words, I was even more flattered by the colleague's response: 'Yes, Pete is very good; he is also very expensive.' WOW. Those words made me the Rolls Royce of writing. I also formed one of my 'sub-drivers: *If a prospective client can't see the value I offer behind that simple statement that connects good with expensive, he or she is too dumb to play in my sandbox and I'd rather work elsewhere.* I've applied that sub-driver several times during my career, always, I'd guess—I'll never know for sure—to my ultimate benefit. Just think of the frustrations I avoided by not working with people who do not value my skills but are also too unaware to know it.

A Costly Misstep: Little did I realize how enmeshed I am in being a one-person entrepreneur when I hired a writer, mainly to take over for me should I ever be unable to work. Several friends and clients warned me not to, 'He cannot write anywhere near as well as you can' (but I can teach him, I replied in my blind stupidity); he comes from a big corporation and works a slower pace (but I can teach him the ways of entrepreneurs), and so on. They were right; I was wrong, and I lost thousands of dollars and my confidence that I knew enough about people to evaluate their abilities.

He, my new writer, accepted an assignment to write a speech for his former boss. He literally spent days studying a subject that he should have known, one of the worst cases of writer's block I have ever witnessed. The client rightly complained that he had not read a draft as the deadline loomed—speeches are one form of communications with realistic deadlines. So I wrote the speech during one of the most gorgeous weekends ever created, when I could have been playing golf. I fired him Monday morning.

I might be a slow learner. A month or so before the speech fiasco this same person had accepted an assignment to write a brochure for a real estate agency. He did with my help, and the client said he was pleased but would not pay our fee for reasons that I still do not fathom but figure that he just wanted to cheat me and I wouldn't sue. This shyster then had the gall to ask us to write other marketing pieces. To my huge amazement, my pseudo writer wanted to accept the work, demonstrating that he did not respect his or my talents. You cannot imagine how quickly I rejected the whole idea with one of my many aphorisms:

All I need to do is hang a sign on my door that shouts 'free writing or training or publishing', and the line of new clients would extend into the next county.

Another of my punditries is to never, with rare exceptions, bet on the come. Promises of future business are usually broken. I say 'usually' because I know that there are times when giving away a sample of your product can open doors to a new client. I wrote a short brochure for a marketing manager of a small company who pleaded that he had spent his budget but would pay me with future business. I naively believed him, he stiffed me and he ignored my phone or email messages. Do you think that he will ever reach competitive supremacy? Or that he would ever practice the Big 4?

The comment that I am very good and very expensive reminds me of a comment from one of my students at Carnegie Mellon University: *'Mr. Geissler taught me more about writing in one semester than I learned in five years of college, but he is a demanding son of a bitch.'* I framed the comment and hung it in my CMU office.

Valuing your talents is far different than living your values, aka your principles. A CEO of a huge manufacturer asked me to write a series of a dozen or so white papers that would explain his stance to employees on important issues such as transforming the company from good to great, and the need to grow revenues and profits to open job opportunities, aka raise the value of his stock options. I agreed to write all the papers except the one on the value of managing for stockholder value, explaining to him that I feel it benefits top execs much more than the troops. In short, it's unfair bull.

The CEO was perplexed. He could not understand how I could forfeit a handsome fee, but also how I could disagree with a principle that he held so dear but I held in such contempt.

A marketing manager in the same company asked me to write a speech on a complex engineering/scientific issue for presentation to a congressional committee, so you can imagine how much the topic had to be condensed and simplified, aka dumbed down. I wrote the speech, my client applauded it for its clarity and concision, and I sent a bill. A few days later my client called and asked that I meet him in his office some 15 miles from mine, I figured so that he would reward my efforts with the next assignment. Not so. When I arrived at his office at the appointed time, he kept me waiting for an hour. Then, when he finally saw me, he pulled my invoice from a desk drawer and said, 'About your bill; it is unacceptable', which I translated to mean 'too high'. (I've never met a client who complained that an invoice was too low, and he was one of two who complained that it was too high.)

I grabbed my bill, tore it up, and said, 'You're right in one respect; it is unacceptable, and I will reissue it. It will be ten percent higher to pay me for the time you wasted. And if you don't pay it in five days, I will tell your boss how you treat suppliers so disrespectfully.' He paid.

When I told this bit of unethical chicanery to others in the same company, they rewarded me with an onslaught of new work. One said: 'It's about time that someone gave that SOB his comeuppance. He ruins our reputations as he ruins his.'

Enjoy being paid and overpaid.

A friend who is a one-person social media guru is busily booking billable hours but absolutely cannot find the time to write and send invoices to his several satisfied customers. It's not that he doesn't have the time; it's that he's afraid to talk about such a personal thing as money, and afraid that he will be rejected or his ego bruised. He does not understand that making money can be fun, creative, and satisfying. It is not shameful, degrading, or, perish the thought, criminal, unethical, or inherently unpleasant.

The VP Marketing of a small financial consulting company asked me to create a new, fresh approach to his ads and other marketing materials. After two hours or so of brainstorming with him, I said that I'd be back to him with some ideas in about a week. I came up with an idea—it's called a 'concept' in the ad business—during the ten-minute stroll back to my office, quickly wrote a one-page proposal/explanation, and put it aside. A week later, I emailed him my proposal and asked for his reaction, knowing that he would approve it enthusiastically.

I waited a week to send my proposal simply because I wanted him to think that I had worked for several days to create it when in fact I had spent three hours, tops. I sent an invoice for creative services for $4000, or more than a thousand dollars an hour, far more than my normal rate. He paid me by return mail, surely the best indication of customer satisfaction and collaboration.

Was I unethical?

Before answering, please consider a famous and perhaps fictitious anecdote about Pablo Picasso. A woman visiting his studio asked him to sketch her caricature, and Pablo did in a few seconds with a few deft strokes of his brush. He then asked for a thousand dollars, and the woman gasped, "For a few seconds work?" To which the master replied, 'Hardly a few seconds; I worked for a lifetime to be able to create that simple drawing.'

I worked for a lifetime to be creative; you did too. Don't you agree that we should be paid well for it?

* *

Value, like beauty, is in the eyes of the beholders: yours and your publics. Enjoy charging for the realistic value you offer your clients, and never ever allow them to intimidate you by demeaning your contribution to their careers. Remember that good suppliers make good clients, and vice versa; it's another win-win, perhaps the biggest in your life. A corollary is that good spouses make good spouses, and good friends ...etc.

DRIVER 6: Adopt These Four Rules for Creating Wealth, For They Are Your Friends

1. **Productive efforts create wealth; unproductive efforts create anxiety and frustration, an extension of work smarter, not harder.** One of my four most active clients—I'll call him Fred—never could figure that out. I first met him at a luncheon and watched in grim amazement as he flitted from subject to subject as if he were a hummingbird in heat or suffered from attention deficit disorder. I'm sure that he thought he was being productive when, in fact, he was being anti-productive. I quickly dubbed him Frenetic Freddie. He is now broke, a result of flitting through three wives and divorces, 52 affairs that he can remember, and more that 50 new cars intended to impress his next affair. He is also sick with a plethora of diseases brought about by too much alcohol and tobacco, which in turn were intensified by his financial and social failures.

BTW, procrastination is another example of unproductive effort—it is wasted effort to put off what you know you shouldn't—and that leads to anxiety. Avoid it.

2. Anyone can enjoy making money and not feel guilty. Most of the miserable people I know drag themselves out of bed and commute to boring jobs, complain about how that are stuck in a rut, and won't do anything to change—the perfect formula for depression. One of my in-rut clients actually resented the pleasure that I derived from my profession, I suppose trying to make me feel guilty; I wouldn't let it happen. He claimed to be not only stuck in a job he hated while working for a boss he loathed, he was stuck in a marriage with a woman he called names that I cannot repeat and she didn't deserve.

He died penniless in a two-room hovel surrounded by empty bottles of booze.

Another top exec I know who admits that his income is in the upper one percent of all earners in America (which I'd guess slots him among the top one hundredth of one percent in the world), yet he complains incessantly about his inconsiderate cohorts, his incompetent bosses, and his need for more money. He stops by my home office on his way to his suburban estate every ten days or so for a drink. He quickly starts to tell me the latest horror story about his job before the front door is closed. When I point out that he is palpably unhappy, he argues that he isn't and cites his OK marriage, effectively changing the subject and proving my point. He then says that he is stuck in his job: 'where else can I earn so much and I need the money and I'll work as long as they pay me.' I predict ulcers and heart attacks.

A related aside: Persons who hate their work/profession/career and who are in it just for the money are probably unhappy and depressed because they cannot perceive options and they have little or no higher meaning in their lives. Yes, they may become rich by working long hours, but they also can become overstressed and eventually suffer the many related physical and mental traumas. I know many people who fit that description—some of my less astute and misguided friends may say that I do—and you probably know several as well, perhaps yourself.

3. **Education does not assure financial success, but that's the way to bet.** A recent article in the local paper compared average incomes and education level of residents in two of Pittsburgh's posh neighborhoods—those with large, well-kept homes and upscale restaurants and stores—with those of two dingy neighborhoods—those with run-down homes and fast-food restaurants and mini markets, at best. Not surprisingly, at least to me, there was a direct cause and effect: Higher education levels equal higher incomes and plusher surroundings. Yes, there are many notable exceptions: Bill Gates and Steve Jobs come immediately to mind. But, again, that is not the way to bet.

If education guaranteed wealth, then professors would be among the wealthiest persons on the planet. And friends of mine with degrees from those fortresses of intellectual pomposity such as Harvard and Carnegie Mellon Universities would be enjoying retirement at ages 64 and 76 respectively instead of fretting over how to pay the mortgage and buy groceries. I've known dozens of people in the same boat.

A friend I met on an extended business trip holds degrees from America's top Ivy League university, and he is the most naive person I know when it comes to money and relationships. He floored me when he said, at age 60, that he planned to retire at 65. I knew that he was broke and I knew that he was going broker every day by living far beyond his annual income of about 200k. I replied, 'If you invested every penny you earn in the next five years—if you don't pay the mortgage or eat or pay taxes—you still cannot retire in five years'. He turned huffy, called me vile names, and decided that we were no longer friends. (He later changed his mind.) Denial is a powerful deterrent to reality.

4. All wealth is created by the human mind, without exceptions. Your intelligence, aka your imagination and creativity, is the only thing you are selling and your only source of income. Think of it as your only marketable asset, or, at the very least, the asset that is your mother lode for all your other assets that you list on your personal and business balance sheets.

Your mind and mine and everybody else's has within it the unique abilities to create new, improved products and services, and to imagine the wants and needs of clients and the effects of decisions, i.e.to 'see' the future, whether what we see turns out to be true or false, real or illusory. Ergo, the path to wealth is to improve the quality of your thinking—to encourage your imagination. To that end, I offer these suggestions:

- **Understand how your mind works.** I adhere to the teachings of The Foundation for Critical Thinking and use many of their concepts and admonishments in my teaching at the university and consultant levels. I am particularly enamored with their insistence that creativity is best understood in simple, everyday thought—it can be demystified—and that critical thinking and creativity are intimately related: 'Creativity without criticality is mere novelty. Criticality without creativity is bare negativity.' Human creativity is a resource that is virtually without limits for the curious mind such as yours. Each of us is creative in our own ways, and each of us can convert our creativity to marketable value.

- **Attend conferences to expand your horizons:** I have attended many conferences sponsored by the electrical and construction industries simply because they are my niche, and I have attended many conferences and posh dinners sponsored by the advertising, public relations, and marketing industry simply because that is where I am pigeon-holed by the SIC codes. I sometimes stray to 'peripheral' conferences such as Creativity and Madness so that I can glimpse into the workings of other minds. BTW, attendance is tax deductible if it contributes to your business.

- **Teach, talk, and tutor at whatever level makes you comfortable and stretches your intelligence, which in my case is college at the undergraduate and graduate levels, and graduates with responsible jobs.** Your primary, overt purpose is to transfer your intelligence to others. Your secondary, covert purpose is to hone your knowledge of your profession by literally forcing you to organize your thinking, and to learn from your students. Yes, teachers learn as much or more from their students as the students learn from their teachers. I extend that ageless thought: good students make good teachers, and vice versa, just as good clients make good suppliers, and vice versa.

I began teaching undergraduates at The University of Pittsburgh, morphed to undergraduates and graduates at Carnegie Mellon University, graduates at Duquesne University, and then to graduates in the working world, some with advanced degrees. Along the way, I lectured to undergraduates at Indiana University of Pennsylvania and to incoming students at several graduate schools of business. I now teach at various consulting firms and speak at their 'lunch and learns', and tutor CEOs and other top execs.

I love the ego-building part of teaching. One of my former graduate students credits me for his career as an engineering manager, still another for her satisfying and lucrative career as an environmental scientist. They and hundreds of others are a big part of my happiness of knowing that I have improved lives.

- Publish, starting with articles in trade magazines and, if you're so inclined, books. You publish for the same reasons that you teach: *to understand and organize your thinking and to broadcast your intelligence.* I started by ghostwriting hundreds of articles for my clients. In essence, I organized and broadcasted my thinking by organizing and broadcasting theirs. I also opened doors with editors who were willing to publish articles under my byline.

The benefits of publishing extend beyond organizing thoughts and broadcasting intelligence; the act of writing for publication, which is far more demanding of good writing skills than writing for an internal or circumscribed audience, creates information, and, therefore, it creates intelligence and literally forces that elusive human talent that we have labeled 'creativity'.

The methodical, evolving disciplined process of writing actually forces new thoughts to emerge from our minds, allowing us to make sense of our surroundings, our lives, and, on a smaller scale, the document that you are composing.

In essence, writing for publication gives our minds a disciplined means of expression and conjuring up that great idea that separates the ordinary from the extraordinary. It is a way to discover what we are thinking. Perhaps E.M. Forster, 1879-1970, the English novelist best known for A Passage to India, said it best: *'How do I know what I think until I see what I write?'*

Charles Darwin agrees, 'I have as much difficulty as ever in expressing myself clearly and concisely; and this difficulty has caused me a great loss of time. But it has the compensating advantage of forcing me to think long and intently about every sentence, and thus I have been led to see errors in reasoning in my own observations or those of others.'

Learn how to compartmentalize, i.e.to concentrate, to focus, solely and intently on the current cerebral matter and eschew all others, and to move seamlessly from one matter to another. Its purpose is to encourage creativity and productivity. Please do not confuse it with multi-tasking, which falsely claims that minds can focus on more than one cerebral task at a time. Its stated purpose is to raise productivity, but in truth it does the opposite. In fact, it guarantees poor performance in several areas rather than success in one.

You can hone your skills at compartmentalizing by combining two cognitive habits: mindfulness (clear-minded awareness of your own mental activity) and mentalizing (paying close attention to what other people are thinking/ saying and are likely to do next). I combine those two habits into the empathy that I address in DRIVER 3.

- Read books written by respected members of your profession, but do not accept their teachings if you disagree. I love Peter Drucker but I also argue with him, as you can see by comments in this book. I also love Chip Conley and his devotion to Maslow's hierarchy of needs and wants, but a friend and fellow author thinks that Conley and Maslow are wrong. You can only imagine our heated, civil discussions. I am one of the many business people who are convinced that Ayn Rand's *Atlas Shrugged* is perhaps the most important business book of last century, and *Fountainhead* is a close second. I distrust business books written by academics who have never managed a business; nevertheless, I admit that some are helpful in abstract ways.

* *

If you buy the idea that your thinking, aka imagination and creativity, is your ultimate source of competitive supremacy, then you will buy the notion that improving your thinking is job one. I've suggested several ways to do that, from studying the tools offered by *The Foundation for Critical Thinking* to exploiting the rigors of good writing. Please use them; it's fun and profitable to watch your mind work.

DRIVER 7: Create Your Own Cozy Conglomerate, For It Is Your Stability

I lived through the conglomerate craze—the merger mania—of the 1960s and 1970s and remember with scary clarity its many failures, among them the infamous demise of Westinghouse, LTV, and ENRON, and the lesser-known demise of two Pittsburgh icons, Dravo and Koppers. The craze was ignited by the management axiom promulgated so confidently by too many business schools: If you can manage one business, you can manage any business. I think of it as the height of arrogance, the root cause of failure. I prefer to think that there are tricks to being successful that are unique to every business.

A small and successful steel fabricator hired me to start a new venture designing and constructing commercial buildings. The new business was to be a new market for fabricated steel as well as a new source of revenue and profit for the parent company. Unfortunately, the culture of the company was such that the owners treated the new business as an afterthought and underfinanced and understaffed it. When the other parts of the company ran into big losses on a bad contract, the owners pulled the plug on the new business, and I joined the ranks of the unemployed.

In the early 1970s, I was in a meeting of Westinghouse engineers and marketers and we were discussing how to communicate the wonders of a new venture into hospital automation. When I asked why Westinghouse was qualified to be in a business so far removed from its core of generating and using electricity—I thought it a stretch that it fits since it would use electricity—I was told that Westinghouse can manage any business. At the time, Westinghouse billed itself as 'The world's most diversified company', as if that were a virtue. In truth, it was a cause of the firm's demise.

I lived a similar story with US Steel. Awash in cash at the time, probably the 1980s, the company's execs decided to enter the business of leasing equipment to other steel companies and manufacturers. I was charged with answering that age-old question—why do business with me?—in a brochure and an article in a trade magazine. I asked the marketing communications manager the question and he said with a straight face: 'Because we are US Steel.' I was expecting something substantive that would benefit customers like lower interest rates or extended payment schedules. I wrote a bunch of pap and my client labeled me a genius.

The three branches of my cozy conglomerate are still operating as I approach my late eighties. I still write marketing material for a few companies, but instead of paper brochures, I write websites and blogs. I still teach, but at consulting firms instead of universities. I still write books and publish them, as well as some authored by others, through my company. I honestly believe that if I stopped I would die of boredom and loneliness in six weeks. Crazy, eh?

Serendipity—being in the right place at the right time for happy results—was the driving force behind my cozy conglomerate, and still is as I write this. Nevertheless, I do not want you to think for a second that careful and formal planning is a waste of time, and that you should be a fatalist. Far from it. Being in the right place at the right time is the essence of planning, as the following anecdotes demonstrate.

I became a professional writer when the owner of the ad agency I inherited while working for the steel fabricator I mentioned above asked me to write a brochure for an engineering company that sold products that he did not understand. I did, he was pleased enough with my prose that he paid me and favored me with a plethora of other assignments. He opened a new market for his firm and I started a new career and the first leg of my conglomerate.

I was helping my soos, at the time a middle manager at a local utility, write a memo to her boss when she stopped and said, 'You have helped me improve my writing, and you can help others'. She noted that her writing class at Penn State focused on creating the Great American Novel, a waste of time for businesspersons, instead of the Simple American Memo. 'Please teach what we need to learn', she pleaded, igniting a chain of serendipitous events.

I called the head of the English Department at the University of Pittsburgh and started to teach undergraduates. A client at Westinghouse recommended me to the head of the English Department at Carnegie Mellon University, and he hired me to teach Advanced Professional and Technical Writing to undergraduate and graduate students. Then a fellow writer recommended me to the head of The Graduate School of Environmental Science and Management, Duquesne University, to develop and teach a new course, Writing for Environmental Professionals. Then a former student at Duquesne, by then a project manager at a large consulting firm, recommended me to his managers to teach writing to scientists and engineers.

His firm became my largest client.

The Expressive Press and the third leg of the cozy conglomerate were born as I was lounging one Saturday morning in my living room. A client from Westinghouse arrived unannounced and handed me a pack of disheveled papers some thee inches high held together by a rubber band, saying, *'The Acquisitions Editor at Quality Press* *tells me that a book is hiding in here, and I should write it but can't. Wanna be a co-author?'*

Of course, I said yes and immediately settled into a comfy chair and scanned the papers, a stream of redundant consciousness that screamed to be edited and reduced by half or more. I did, the book became a publisher's bestseller, and my client and I embarked on a sequel (which I am fond of saying is an attempt to imitate yourself). The second book didn't sell, but it launched my career as a an author first and a publisher second.

**

Each of us has core competencies around which we can build related competencies; mine is words. I label a friend and client as 'the ultimate engineer'. He has expanded his expertise to include testifying at trials where engineering is an issue. Another friend and client, an HR manager, plays guitar and sings at local bistros, a rare but successful departure from his core competencies; he says the gigs keep him sane and pay a good part of one child's college education.

DRIVER 8: Avoid Greed At All Costs, For Greed Is Self-Defeating

Be aware of your capacity: Overbooking—accepting work that is beyond your capacity to deliver the final product, is one sure way to go out of business. The reason: chances are that the quality of the product isn't up to your standard—you compromise quality in order to make a delivery date, for example—and you usually deliver late. In essence, you violate the three characteristics of a salable product and competitive supremacy: quality, cost, and schedule.

When I told a VP of a nationwide engineering firm that over booking was one route to failure, he looked at me in amazement, which is understandable. He had spent his entire 30-year career beating the bushes for the next contract, a trait of the consulting business and, for that matter, any business that survives through an unbroken series of assignments, as my writing business does but my publishing business does not.

When I was younger and hungrier, I accepted almost every and any assignment that fit my expertise. I felt then that I had the energy and drive to handle what I call 'creative overload' and it worked for a few years to build my wealth but also to erode my health. It does not work now that I am more mature and, I hope, wiser.

A respected printing salesman was in my office one day and watched as I frantically juggled phone calls from clients and questions from my assistant. During a lull in the action, he predicted that I would be dead soon from the pressure. I disagreed with one of my many aphorisms: 'Busyness won't kill me or anybody. The stress from busyness will, and I have none since I love what I do. *The trick is to be calm despite chaos, to not lose your composure while others are losing theirs.*'

My four major clients—communications managers from Fortune 500 companies and one smaller firm—recognized that they and I would benefit if my workload was more steady, and called a meeting to discuss it. I think of the meeting as unique in the annals of business; I haven't heard of any arrangement like it before or since, although retainers come close. We jointly decided that the solution was to plan and communicate: They would project their needs for my services for a year and alert me a month in advance of reasonable starting dates. I would alert all four when I saw an overload or underload on the horizon and they could delay or accelerate starting dates to fill in the lows and shave the highs.

Then the law of unintended consequences kicked in. One of my Big Four needed a series of speeches for his CEO and a few EVPs, none of which were in the original plan. I went into overload for overpay—don't you love the conection? —and again emerged richer, more appreciated, more in demand by this particular group, and more exhausted. I was rewarded for my generosity with my time with their generosity with cash, applause, and loyalty. I also left without three other clients who found other suppliers for assignments that they had planned to be mine, so I wonder if I came out ahead or behind after this episode of overbooking and, let's face it, greed.

Insourcing is another sure way to go out of business, and it stems from egomania and its cousin, an inability to recognize and admit that your abilities and time are limited. Entrepreneurs are by nature stubborn and independent. They tend to think that they can do everything needed to operate their business, when they can't either well or efficiently. They avoid spending the money for specialists who, for example, can keep the books and order supplies. It's destructive, stinkin' thinkin'.

I often advise my clients in the top levels of corporate America that it pays to hire me to write their marketing materials, especially their speeches. Not only are my speeches better in many ways than those that they write for themselves, they cost less since they are free to do what they do best—manage and lead—and I do what I do best - write and think. They understand the dynamics and economics of outsourcing.

I take my own advice. My second decision when I started my business was to hire a trusted assistant to take care of myriad details such as invoicing and bookkeeping and, at the time, word processing. (My first decision, for those who are curious, was to lock in my clients.) I subsequently retained an accountant to placate the IRS and its several sister groups at various levels of government, a management consultant when I decided to expand my client base and raise my fees, and then a money manager when I started to earn more than I spent and could invest the excess.

I could have done all the tasks that they did but, what a waste of my talents! On top of that, I learned a lot by working with the experts in other fields. For example, the management consultant noted quite perceptively that I was billing an exceptional number of hours. So he invoked that well-known law of business: raising prices might lose a client or two, but surely not all, and my income would not change. In short, I would work less for the same or more revenue...

...which is exactly what happened, almost. I raised my prices by 25 percent and not one of my clients noticed or, if they did, my niche was so strong they didn't care. I ended up billing the same number of hours and earning 25 percent more, giving more reason to retain a money manager, which I did 25 years ago as I write this. At the time, I was juggling some 45 financial reports from a dozen banks and brokers and reading the Wall Street Journal to get some insight into investments. What I really got was week-old rumors and hours of wasted, unproductive time.

Enter my financial manager. When I first contacted him, I asked for three references and he laughed and said that he would, but let's be real, they would be his most satisfied clients. I agreed, called all three and got the expected applause. I will never forget a physician's comment, 'I could not have retired without Jim Browne.'

I met recently with Jim and thanked him for all his help in increasing my wealth but also—perhaps equally important—to raise my productivity, comfort, and peace of mind, which of course raised my income. He is a big reason that I live comfortably, and I recognize that I paid him well for that. As we parted, I reminded him of the physician's comment of twenty-five years ago—it was my deja vu all over again—and said in total appreciation, 'I could not retire without you.' He, with his customary humility, said, 'You could have done it without me.' He was wrong.

Now, before moving on, I want to explain that I enjoyed an especially strong niche in the business of marketing communications based on my education in science, engineering, and finance, and experience in engineering/construction. 'A unique combination for a writer', according to one of my clients. I often describe myself as a 'reformed engineer', and the most fortunate freelancer in history.

My niche was so strong that the business development people at this city's largest ad agency, during their regular state-of-the-art meetings, would discuss my abilities to book business that they wanted and felt they deserved. According to my mole, aka industrial spy (every small business can benefit from having one) they couldn't figure out why, yet, in perhaps the perfect contradiction, they preached the virtues of positioning and branding but did not recognize mine.

My niche was a weak sister compared to that of a small, 15-person electrical engineering firm founded by a friend who is also a contributor to my book on dignity. He is also one very smart electrical engineer and businessman who has cornered the market for design of electrical systems in commercial and university buildings in Western and Central Pennsylvania. He told me recently that a client dubbed him, 'the only game in town'.

The bottom line is this: **I created an intelliniche oligopoly, and my engineer friend created an intelliniche monopoly...of course within a small geographic area**

and skill set. I doubt that the anti-trust folks in DC care, but you might.

* *

Beware of overbooking and insourcing; they indicate greed and short-term thinking that could very well erode your reputation as a responsible, intelligent supplier, just what you do not want. Instead, think longer term and be confident that your appreciative clients will continue to collaborate with you and feed you contracts and cash.

DRIVER 9: Be Creative When Planning Your Future, For It Is Your Roadmap

Seneca, the Roman philosopher and statesman who lived more than 2000 years ago, could very well have been thinking about business in the 20th and 21st centuries when he said,' Our plans miscarry because they have no aim. If one does not know to which port one is sailing, any wind is the right wind.'

In today's lingo, he said that if you don't know where you're going, you can't get there. I can only imagine the vast amounts of time and money that were wasted in Seneca's day by sailing in wrong directions to wrong destinations, or, today, in working toward the wrong or vague goals, or no goals at all.

A Costly Misstep: I lost my way, my winds were wrong, when I invested in a restaurant, a business that I knew nothing about and still don't. My misguided voyage started when I became friendly with the manager of a chain restaurant and I actually began to like the guy, a fatal flaw in many business dealings. Anyway, one day he approached my soos and I as we were enjoying Sunday brunch and out came the magic words:

'How'd you like to invest in a restaurant?'

I lit up with the passion of the naive, aka stupid, and asked for details. After all, I had spent so much time in restaurants and bars that I thought I could run one. The perfect arrogant non sequitur.

I ate up the details: 'A destination, white table cloth place called Wright's Seafood Inn. Been in business for almost a century, now for sale ...etc' I knew the place, had eaten there a few times, liked it, and bit for a bunch of bucks. My soos sat quietly as the owner set the hook.

She wasn't quiet when we left the restaurant. 'Don't invest anything that you can't afford to lose,' she advised.' And do not invest with this guy. He is bringing in his current squeeze to help manage the place and she has never held a job above server at a chain restaurant and check-out girl at the local supermarket. Mixing raw sex with business is never good business. Remember the inkwell.'

My chutzpa, that wonderfully descriptive Jewish word for unbridled arrogance, took over my sense. Not only did I invest, I brought in another investor. To shorten a long, sordid tale, the owner lied about the amount of money he had attracted—even named a few local athletes who promised cash but didn't come up with any—and didn't know how to manage a restaurant that wasn't a chain where someone else works the details like menu, purchasing, and accounting.

The business folded within a year for two primary reasons that are far too common: lack of working capital, and arrogant, 'I'm the smartest guy in the room' management that Jeffrey Skillings of ENRON popularized. I lost my investment, which was bad enough, but even worse was that I am still guilty about bringing in another investor. Amazingly, he is still my friend and I hope he has forgiven me for my transgressions. Perhaps more amazingly, my soos no longer says 'I told you so.' No wonder I love her.

While sailing for the wrong port is one failure of planning; another is thinking short term—which I am convinced is the business and societal disease of our time. Companies that are managed solely or primarily for the next quarter's financial results—the ultimate in short term thinking that does not rise to the level of planning—often aren't sustainable. I should know: I lived through two.

I was enjoying an after-golf libation with a marketing VP at my largest client company and we discussed planning. He said, 'Long range planning at our company ends with the next coffee break.' Another exec with the same company said, 'We spend huge amounts of time and money—much of it for consultants' fees—to create plans that satisfy our top execs and board that we are thinking about the future.

Then we put the voluminous documents, some hundreds of pages of text and graphs that nobody reads, on the shelf to gather dust and we turn our attention to putting out the latest fire.'

That company, once a household name, is no longer in business. Many insiders blame its bankruptcy on a planning process that focused on financial goals rather than on such long-term considerations as R&D, personnel development, and ethics. The process looked good on paper: managers projected three scenarios: best, worst, and likely, so the graphs were impressively complex, far too complex for board members to do anything more than glance at them and, perhaps, scan the captions.

The CEO of another client, an engineering/construction firm with a century-long history of competence in one industry, made the arrogant error called 'line extension' by thinking that the same competencies could be transferred to another industry. The CEO, an accountant/ lawyer whose compensation was tied to stock price, aka quarterly earnings, figured that if his engineers could design and build one type of industrial plant, they could do the same for any type. Not so: As I learned many years ago, there are tricks to every trade, and transferring tricks from one trade to another varies between difficult to impossible, and is always expensive.

A friend and early mentor grew unhappy with working for a large civil engineering company and started his own. He prospered and his company soon grew to almost 300 employees. Then arrogance, greed, obsession, and a massive dose of stubbornness kicked in. He fell into 'line extension' and started a new business in materials processing engineering and invested heavily in it before he realized that his engineers were unable to deliver the quality design expected by his clients. His entire company went bankrupt, disrupting the lives of hundreds of employees and even more spouses and children.

My first accountant tried repeatedly to convince me that I needed a monthly statement so that I'd know exactly how I was doing, down to the last penny. Bull. I knew in my bones how I was doing—good, bad, indifferent were close enough to reality for me—and I didn't need to know the exact numbers. I settled for a yearly statement, and wouldn't have done even that if the IRS would accept my best estimates. BTW, I fired my first accountant who I thought was using me to finance his retirement, and hired another who actually listened to me and understood the simplicity of my business.

Planning starts by stating your purposes(s) in life, as you learned in Driver 1, and then asking yourself: How do I meet my purpose(s)? What must I do to live the life that I want? Do I have the intellectual and other resources to convert ideals to reality?

My planning process considers the short term of one year, and the longer term of my productive life, which early in my career was decades, and now, at 85, is a hoped-for three years. My process is simple and is based on a favorite book, ***Creative Breakthroughs.*** The author espouses that you write—not just think—on the far left side of a long piece of paper where you are in all phases of your life, in essence, your profile. I think of my life in two parts, professional and social, then in as many subparts as I can imagine.. For example, under professional I write the three legs of my cozy conglomerate: writing, teaching, and publishing.

Then, on the far right side, I write those same words, phrases and sub phases as I want them to be, not as they are. They become my goals. I try to avoid goals that are probably out of my reach, that exceed my realistic expectations, such as writing the Great American Novel or teaching at Harvard Business School. Big companies that I've worked with call them 'stretch goals', a euphemism that I don't think fools employees who, quite realistically, think of them as impossible to reach and, therefore, reasons for managers to avoid raises and bonuses.

Then—and here's the tough part—I write in the middle what I need to do to move from the left to right sides—my action plan, my to-do or bucket list or, in the parlance of big business and the military, my tactics.

I'm sure that you think you know the direction of your business and life, including your tactics, without going to all the trouble of writing it; I am equally sure that you do not know your plans in any cohesive detail, or that writing your plans will actually clarify your thinking and create new knowledge.

It will. I am a firm believer that writing is the one way to clear your thinking, *if the writer adheres to the disciplines of the language.*

I am echoing many esteemed writers with that pivotal thought. William Zinser said, in his book *Writing To Learn:* 'Clear writing is the logical arrangement of thought.' Susan Horton says, in her book. *Thinking Through Writing,* that '...this book is not so much how to write ...but how writing works, how your mind works... it is a kind of 'watch yourself think' book.'

I had an 'aha' moment early in my career as a professional writer. I discovered that the execs for whom I wrote speeches and other marketing materials were less interested in my peerless words than they were in my forcing them to think about their words, what they were saying to their publics. One came right out and said that my value to him was to help him think by asking, 'do you really want to say that to this audience?'

One result of my 'aha' moment was that I espouse a definition of writing that is becoming popular:

Information in, enlightenment out.

Information is the raw material, while enlightenment is the finished product.

Intelligence is the catalyst for making the transition from information to enlightenment.

An example: The CEO of my major client retained me to write an important speech and, when we met in his office, he handed me an outline and said, 'Here are the main points I want to make.' I knew this bigshot well enough to know that I could tamper with his outline if I could defend my tampering with solid, sensible reasons, aka thinking.

I did more than tamper; I restructured and rewrote. The CEO read it and said, 'this doesn't follow my outline.'

'Yes, but this is much better', and explained why. He reluctantly agreed and, after he gave the speech, called to tell me that I was right and to thank me for making him a star. Good clients make good suppliers, etc., and ain't humility grand!

* *

Formal planning is a prerequisite for successful businesses of any size; it literally forces analytical thinking that can uncover problems and opportunities that can be missed by merely thinking about the future. You can fit your planning process into any one of many available templates, or you can build your own.

DRIVER 10: Retain Financial Advisers You Can Trust, For They Are Your Security

Your trusted accountant and investment adviser are major keys to your success. They need to cooperate among themselves and with you, the head of the three-person team and their source of income. The team's primary goal is to free your time to do what you do best: manage your business and life to create wealth and happiness. Your supporting goals are to maximize return on your investments and your business/intellect, minimize taxes (as important as maximizing returns for creating wealth), and to stay out of the clutches of the IRS and its many brethren, a benefit that I need to clarify.

The IRS randomly selected me for an audit as part of their program to profile businesses of various sizes and types. The auditor arrived at my office early every morning for a week and examined my records down to the last client lunch. She handed me a list of 20-25 questions and requests for more information when she left around noon. All had to be answered by my accountant by the next morning. Her report said that she had never examined a more complete and clear set of books, a tribute to my assistant and accountant. Despite such accolades, I, not the IRS, had to pay my accountant more than ten thousand dollars. I shudder to think what his fees would have been if I had been accused of some misdeed. BTW, the auditor was extraordinarily polite, professional, and unthreatening, a far and pleasant cry from the stereotype.

Your team can help you make one of your first and more important decisions; are you a corporation or a sole proprietor. I started as a regular corporation to separate and protect my business and personal assets and to maximize contributions to my pension plan, which in turn minimizes personal and business taxes.

A quick story to demonstrate the inanities of corporate law: At the time, Pennsylvania required a three-person board of directors to register the firm as a corporation. I quickly appointed two of my core clients VPs and directors. Then, the day Pennsylvania approved my application, I, the CEO, called a special meeting of the board and fired my two VPs for not attending. In essence, I became a sole proprietor with the benefits of being a corporation.

Changes in the tax codes soon eliminated those benefits, and I reverted to a sole proprietorship, mainly to simplify my tax returns and minimize fees paid to my accountant. Perhaps you will be surprised to know that my accountant agrees that minimizing his fees is good for all three of us: He benefits with a happy client who has referred several of his friends to him, I benefit with a higher income, and my manager benefits with more cash to invest. I think of it as a fine example of Customer Collaboration and a win-win-win.

My five rules for building a trusted team:

1. First and foremost: Never, ever retain a friend or relative to be your accountant or manager despite pressure to do so. You either cannot fire them, or you will hesitate to fire or critique them if you are dissatisfied with their service for any reason. Guilt and family/friendship ties are powerful motivators to maintain the status quo despite problems. A close friend worked as a financial manager with a large firm and wanted to handle my growing account. He went so far as to put together a detailed proposal. I turned him down, pleading that he was close to retiring and I did not want to change advisers so soon. The real reason was our friendship, which somehow survived.

2. Retain an accountant whose clients are similar in size as your business. My first accountant was a large firm with an impressive roster of Fortune 500 clients. Not only were the fees excessive, the service from a careless and incompetent novice/trainee was so sloppy that I was constantly fixing their errors, sure signs that I was an afterthought. I soon found a two-person firm that was recommended by a mutual friend and client, and my fees and irritations dropped by 90 percent. I am not kidding. I have been with that firm and the same two people for 21 years. Good clients make good suppliers.

3. Never retain a stockbroker or his/her firm to manage your money. Stockbrokers will tell you that they are money managers when they are really sellers of investments recommended by their analysts, most of whom are staring at computer screens in ivory towers in NYC poring over statistics and polls. My first and last broker, a rare and honest bird who knew this, pointed out that analysts' recommendations rarely made money and the firm's mutual funds were underperformers. He suggested an independent manager in California, minimizing his commissions and eventually losing my account via his honesty.

I had only one issue with my manager in California: we could never look each other in the eye and develop the close relationship that I wanted with a person who would influence my life in such profound ways. I searched for a new, nearby manager for almost a year before I found one with compatible, modest values. My search started with my insurance agent, whose company's fees and press releases exceeded its performance. I looked into three large mutual fund groups and was happy with their fees but felt—perhaps unfairly—that they would invest in their own funds even if they were not in my best interests. I eventually interviewed a nearby firm and individual and have been with him for 25 years as I write this, with no intention of changing. We have grown together, another win-win.

BTW, I trust him and his associates so explicitly that I authorize him to make all of my financial decisions without my input, but he insists that I am involved so that I understand his reasoning for even minor changes in my portfolio. I appreciate his concerns but, in fact, I usually 'rubber stamp' his recommendations, another indication of my trust and his empathy with my needs.

4. **Stop reading the WSJ, NYTimes, and any stock tip-sheets; that is the job of your team if they so choose.** You will save hours a day that you can devote to your business. When people ask me what I did when I first hired my manager, I reply that I cancelled all my subscriptions to financial rags, starting with the WSJ. Not that the WSJ and others aren't valuable, it's just that they have little value for you as you concentrate on building your business.

5. **Retain your accountant as soon as you start your business, and your manager as soon as you are earning more that you spend.** Do not wait until you think your account is big enough to attract competent advisers. Many will recognize a rising financial star, and take you on. My manager, for example, accepted me as a client when I was relatively poor, and now manages my growing portfolio,

plus the portfolios of two of my four children and a dozen or so of my friends.

* *

I know so many people who have ruined their lives through financial abuse that I plan to write a book about them, the working title of which is a polite How to Ransack Your Life. Most have earned considerably more than I have, and all have frittered away their earnings, are broke in their old age, and wonder why. They needed to read this book years ago. Pity.

The lives of these misguided souls have been directed by such self-centered and self-justifying non sequiturs as 'you only live once, so you might as well live it up', and 'life is short; make the most of it'. While the first phrases of these old saws are indisputably true, the second are so squishy that they cry out for further insight. Just what is 'live it up?' or 'make the most of it?'

One subject for Ransack was a couple who interpreted 'live it up' to mean so many party-boat trips that they set a record that the boat company highlighted in its newsletter. They justified the cost as 'not as much as you'd think', which really is 'I have no idea'. They died almost penniless living in a home that their son described as 'a hovel in need of extensive repair'.

Another is a man who, when he was earning $300k a year, thought 'making the most of it' as buying shoes that cost $400 a pair, four leather belts when he needed only one, and muscle cars that idle on the freeways. He is now, at age 63, sponging off his friends and earning about one-fifth of what he did.

I interpret 'to make the most of it' far differently: to live responsibly and comfortably—I do not think that the two are mutually exclusive—and to live the drivers in this book, to live as carefree and independently as possible. One of my personal aphorisms for responsible living is:' If I (you) want to be happy and prosperous, live to stay out of the medical and legal systems; I (you) can't afford either.' The implications are so immense that I need to write another book to explain them.

* *

Find an accountant and asset manager that you can trust by interviewing at least three and then interviewing their clients with businesses and goals similar to yours. Be sure that your accountant and manager can work together, i.e. that they do not have a history of conflict and respect each other.

DRIVER 11: Nurture Your Most Important Asset: Your Mind and Body, for They are Your Critical Foundations

My sense is that virtually all people striving for wealth and happiness, most of them committed entrepreneurs, find it difficult to go on vacation, especially to leave their homes and other familiar places. I am one of them. Perhaps I am thwarted by the knowledge that a vacation costs entrepreneurs twice or more than it costs an employee. Entrepreneurs must add the cost of lost income to the cost of the vacation; nobody pays them for lollygagging on the beach, golf course, or Sushi bar.

I am convinced that the counter-argument that 'everyone needs to get away and recharge' is a hoax perpetrated by homebound spouses and the travel industry. Nobody truly 'gets away' these days. For proof, you need only to witness beachcombers tapping on their laptops and talking on their smart phones. Not long ago a client and I were playing golf at my club and we picked up another twosome. One of them was so self-important that he could not turn off his phone, apologizing at every disturbing ring that he was negotiating a big deal of some sort, as if I cared. When his phone rang while I was putting I explained that I could not enjoy the game under these rather unpleasant circumstances and asked him to play with another twosome for the back nine. Honestly, he verified his lack of empathy by looking hurt and perplexed.

I've noticed also that when people return from a trip they invariably say how good it is to be home, that the best part of a trip is returning to the old familiar stomping grounds. I know that I feel that way. When I deplaned after three weeks in Hawaii on a lucrative business trip, I was so relieved I actually kissed the tarmac, and then couldn't find my car in a lot full of look-a-likes. A manager at the local hotel saw me and helped me; if she hadn't, I may still be looking.

Anyway, if the best leg of a trip is to arrive home, and I agree with so many of my friends that it is, then why go? And why go if you enjoy your work so much that you think of it as play? I do, and have for years.

Now, before you label me a curmudgeon, killjoy or worse who is destined for a heart attack and ulcers, I am fully aware that 'getting away' for two weeks or longer to relax and leave the rat race could be important, even necessary, for you and your family. No question that you likely need to unload your stress and broaden your outlook on life, and no question that your spouse and kids need to as well. I've known too many marriages go bust, too many people of both sexes turn to booze and affairs to relieve stress, when one partner becomes too enmeshed in business. So much has been written and spoken about a 'balanced life' that I won't add to the din.

I have solutions, one unreal, one real. On the unreal side, just turn off your computer and cell phone. Won't happen; most of us work 24/7/365.

My real solution is to create a getaway vacation at home, which isn't as much of a contradiction as you may think. My soos and I do just that for a week or two by scheduling an event such as a play or concert for at least every other day, and a lunch or dinner at a new-to-us restaurant every day. We treat ourselves with special wines that we might not ordinarily buy, and we take care of our businesses (she is a one-person accounting firm) for one hour early every morning, then turn off the computer and phone unless a real crisis is pending.

We enjoy the best of two worlds by getting away by staying home.

Just as vacations cost entrepreneurs twice as much as they cost employees, so does becoming ill and not able to work. Therefore, it pays to stay healthy, and I know how simplistic that may sound.

Statistics show that entrepreneurs miss fewer days of work than employees miss. One reason beyond cost is that entrepreneurs don't typically publish policies that allow a certain number of sick days, which always seemed to me to invite days off whether the employee is sick or not. In essence, the large employer is awarding vacation days to healthy employees who call in sick anyway. I've always found that to be dishonest; others find it to be just another perk.

So, aside from thanking your parents for the genes that keep you healthy, you can behave as if your body and mind are your most important assets, without which you cannot earn a dime or be happy.

First, you need a four-person team of a doctor, dentist, chiropractor, and you, all of whom believe in and practice prevention, not cure. I remember an ad for, ironically, a defunct brand of cigarettes that touted their superior tobacco as 'an ounce of prevention is worth a pound of cure'. My chiropractor is fond of expressing the same thought differently: 'It's simpler and less costly to stay well than it is to become well.'

You are the leader, the CEO, of your health team, just as you are the leader of your financial team. Your duties are to communicate clearly and concisely your needs and wants so your specialists can meet them most efficiently. Your financial and health teams share the same goals: to maximize your productivity, income, and happiness, one to manage the health of your financial assets, the other the health of your primary asset from which all other assets emanate: your body and mind.

Self-appointed gurus have written and spoken millions of words about health, and the common and overarching threads are to control your weight and increase your energy by eating a proper diet, exercising more, and avoiding alcohol and tobacco. I will not add to the din. Instead, I'll address why you should listen to me, a man without medical credentials, and then a few opinions and habits that work.

I am 85 years young, as the cliche goes, and proud of it. My vitals are akin to those of a professional athlete, and I have gained only one-third of a pound per year during the past 65 years, or about 20 pounds. My PCP of twenty years is happy with my weight, saying that it is 'not unhealthy.' a double negative that might mean 'it's healthy', but I do not believe it and constantly strive to lose ten pounds, mainly so my clothes fit better and I am more energetic. When my PCP enters the examination room for my six-month checkup, his first words are, 'what can't I do for you today?' To which I invariably reply, 'nothing, I hope. I'm good to go.' 'I hope that we have that repartee for the remainder of my life, and that you can with your PCP as well.

Here are a few opinions and habits that might help:

- Find the PCP who is also into sports medicine. My first PCP was the exercise guru for the Pittsburgh Steelers and one of the doctors who ran onto the field should a player be hurt. He was also a silver medalist in the Olympics. He believes in fitness. The result was a fitness program designed specifically for me that I still follow 40 years later. When my first PCP retired, I interviewed several replacements and selected one who knew and respected my first and agreed with his prevention approach. He is also one of those rare MDs who listen to understand, another form of empathy.

- Find a PCP who knows their limitations and will refer you to a specialist when needed. Mine referred me to a world-renowned prostate cancer specialist when he detected a suspicious trend. The happy result was a quick and painless fix.

- Find a dentist and chiropractor who understand prevention, not an easy task.

- Walk everywhere you can.

- Do not join a health club for two reasons. They waste valuable time traveling to and from, changing clothes, and showering, and I often think that they prefer that you keep coming back rather than resign when you meet your conditioning goals. Instead...

- Create a gym/exercise space in your home and/or office. I have a treadmill desk that I hop on when I'm stuck on a long phone call or when I need to read, and I have an elliptical for heavier cardio workouts. They are complemented by weights. Just as important, I installed a top- level home theater in my exercise room to prevent boredom by watching a movie or a sports event.

- Create a routine that fits your lifestyle. I try to work out every day at 6PM, when I'm quite certain I can find a movie on the home theater.

- Exercise your mind by working on crossword, Soduko, or similar puzzles and by reading books and magazines that stretch your thinking.

* *

Your most important assets are your healthy mind and body; only if you nurture them can you exploit your other most important asset, your intelligence and creativity. Those assets complement each other to be the closest manifestations of your life that I can imagine.

DRIVER 12: Select The Vehicle You'll Ride into Entrepreneurship, For It Will Influence Your Wealth and Happiness

You are faced with only three vehicles for your drive to wealth and happiness, and the three are mutually exclusive; you can't be more than one, and your decision might set a course for a lifetime. (Sounds like marriage, right?).

Your first option, being an employee, is the least likely to lead to prosperity. Employers tell employees how much they can make based on guidelines they set, often in collusion with a consultant. Employers tend to offset this limiting factor by selling the security of a large group but, in my experience, that is a cruel illusion. I worked for a large engineering/construction firm for six years and recall the HR manager telling me, 'you'll make a competitive salary that will allow you to live comfortably but not lavishly (aka 'You'll never get rich working here.'), but you'll always have a job'. The company filed for bankruptcy some ten years later, a victim of bad decisions made by greedy management, and thousands of employees were on the street.

Being an intrepreneur—a hybrid of employee and entrepreneur—is your second option, and is best illustrated by example. I worked for a short time for a company as a sales engineer that paid a small salary and substantial bonuses for increasing revenue, and huge bonuses for increasing profits. Several sales people refused promotions because their bonuses were larger than their salaries would be as executives. In essence, they were entrepreneurs operating within a fragile cocoon provided by a generous employer.

Your income as an employee, even an intrepreneur, is at best a springboard to being an entrepreneur. I admit to a strong bias: When people ask me what happened when I went into business for myself, I quickly and facetiously say, 'I became happy and modestly affluent, in that order.' What more could I or anyone ask for? I was ready after eighteen years as an employee, too often as a victim of management that I could not respect and often thought of self-serving idiots, to be polite. In short, I figured I could do better—be happier and live more meaningfully—on my own. I was ready to leave the illusory cocoon and:

•   **Be happy in my love of words and freedom.** When I showed my resume to a friend a few years before I became an entrepreneur, he saw that I had been employed by a succession of smaller companies. Entrepreneurship, a one-person enterprise, was the inevitable result.

- **Earn whatever amount my time and talents would allow.** One year, while working for a large engineering construction company, I negotiated projects equal to 70 percent of the firm's revenue and was rewarded with a 5% raise by a boss who admitted that he didn't have the slightest clue what I did. I was so angry that I went immediately to a local bar to quell the ire, became beyond tipsy, and reevaluated my life. I realized then that my income as an employee depends more on company policy and personal bias than on the quantity and quality of my work—was a puppet whose strings were controlled by unknown and unseen forces. On a positive note, perhaps it was a tipping point and I should thank my idiot boss.

- **Be confident that my income would rise and appreciative clients would always employ me.** My confidence was bolstered by knowing that small businesses create some 80 percent of new jobs and I would be one of them, and some 70 percent of millionaires in America work for themselves, 20% are retired, and 10% work for someone else. I looked forward to joining the 70 percent.

Perhaps you do too.

* *

Nobody realizes more than I do that leaving the so-called security of a large organization can be traumatic simply because so many of us have been reared and brain washed to think that bigger is safer. Perhaps it was the route to the good life in another era; I do not think it is now.

EPILOGUE: You're In the Driver's Seat

I wrote this book to share insights into a fulfilled life, hoping that others who are similarly inclined will follow my lead. To that end, the book is both a description of a life and prescription for other lives, perhaps yours.

If Freud was correct, if a bit simplistic, when he said that happiness is good love and good work, then I am not at all surprised that I am amazingly happy and have been for years. I attribute my grin to being in love with my soos, work, and the people I work with, many of whom are my closest friends.

Readers looking for overnight success will not find it here. Instead, they will find twelve drivers that work singly or synergistically over the longer haul. They can help you fulfill the vast promises of free enterprise and entrepreneurship to help you take charge of your life, your income, and your happiness.

I am a big fan—with the caveats below—of free enterprise, aka self-reliance, laissez faire economics, and that dirty word capitalism. I am a fan first because it has been good to me, and I hope that it will be as good to you. I am a fan also because I read Ayn Rand's masterpiece of prophesy, *Atlas Shrugged*, in my early twenties more than 60 years ago, and still think it is the best business book ever, the best homage to individualism in the guise of her 'ideal man'. I agree with Winston Churchill: *'Some see private enterprise as a predatory target to be shot, others as a cow to be milked, but few see it as a sturdy horse pulling a wagon.'*

Then, in my early forties, now almost 45 years ago, I read **The Lessons of History,** by Will and Ariel Durant. In its Chapter IX, Socialism and History, the authors say: 'The capitalist, of course, has fulfilled a creative function in history: He has gathered the savings of the people into productive capacity by the promise of dividends or interest; he has financed the mechanization of industry and agriculture and the rationalization of distribution. The result has been such a flow of goods from producer to consumer as history has never before seen. He has put the liberal gospel of liberty to his use by arguing that businessmen left relatively free from transportation tolls and legislative regulation can give the public a greater abundance of food, homes, comfort, and leisure than has ever come from industries managed by politicians, manned by government employees, and supposedly immune to the laws of supply and demand.'

The same ideas are expressed negatively and darkly by those other great books of prophesy, ***Brave New World,*** by Aldous Huxley, and ***1984,*** by George Orwell.

And now, before you think of me as an unfeeling zealot, my caveats: Pure free enterprise has failed to meet the first and primary goal of governments: to provide for everyone's happiness, with all sorts of sub-goals such as to provide for defense, health, and transportation.

I think that government, complemented mainly by business, can meet those goals by with a hybrid of free enterprise, one that is more flexible and humane, more generous. Let's call it Generous Free Enterprise.

A first step would be to tap the generosity of business, especially small business, to share their skills and money. I think that taxes on those of us who are living large should be raised by, say, ten to fifteen percent, and the money used to improve the living standards of the less fortunate and less talented, and to improve our infrastructure and health care. I propose that despite my deep distrust that government at any level is able to spend/invest money as responsibly of beneficially as private citizens or organizations.

Perhaps I take this stand because I know of a family who through no fault of their own has come on hard times and cannot afford medicine for a teen child with a genetic disease. I am not proud of an America that allows deserving people to suffer or die because they cannot afford medicine or other goods needed to sustain life.

I do not think that socialism or its awful bother, communism, are the answers; both systems are blemished with a long history of failure and human misery. I invite you to read more in *Lessons*.

This Little Black Book is not the place for an extended debate on the merits of various economic systems. It is the place to point out that the one system that supports entrepreneurship most avidly is free enterprise. We are fortunate to be living in it, or the closest system to it that I know of, and we are fortunate to have the opportunity to tweak it to be better than ever. Yes, I know that the democratic socialism of some Scandinavian countries, the consensus politics of Japan, the state-sponsored growth of South Korea, and more recently the communism in China, support free enterprise.

Twenty or so years ago I hosted a woman from Ukraine who traveled to America to study free enterprise and entrepreneurship. She owned a knitting and gift shop that she felt could grow and be more prosperous. One morning I drove her to a Home Depot, a Bed, Bath. and Beyond, and a huge and upscale supermarket. As we traveled and toured these opulent stores, her eyes widened in amazement and disbelief. She said what I already suspected:'Your economic system is much better that ours.'

A closing remark from *Lessons*: 'The fear of capitalism has compelled socialism to widen freedom, and the fear of socialism has compelled capitalism to increase equality. East is East and West is West, and soon the twain will meet.'

Perhaps the meeting will be at Generous Free Enterprise.

* *

Any sentient, curious, and upwardly mobile person can reap the rewards and benefits of entrepreneurship. Count your blessings that you live with free enterprise and that it encourages your financial and social success. Let's hope that it will soon be Generous Free Enterprise.

PETE'S PUNDITRY: Words To Play By

Busyness won't kill or harm anybody. The stress from busyness will, and I have none since I love what I do. I hope that you do too. The trick is to be calm despite chaos, to maintain your composure while others are losing theirs.

Generosity—the willingness to give money, time, and other assets to people who do not need them—begets generosity; prosperity begets prosperity is a corollary.

Happiness is aligning your expectations with your abilities to meet them; lowering your expectations to below your abilities will lead to disappointment; raising them to above your abilities will lead to frustration and anger. A related thought: The only purpose in life is to enjoy it. I am echoing Santayana, who said,

'There is no cure for birth and death, save to enjoy the interval.'

Ralph Waldo Emerson said that 'It is a luxury to be understood.' I disagree: It is a necessity to be understood for everyone who aspires for financial and social success.'

The faster I work, the longer the job takes. Fixing errors made in haste takes longer than not making mistakes in the first place. Measure twice, cut once. The same is true of health.

Good clients make good suppliers, and vice versa. The client/supplier relationship could be the ultimate symbiosis.

Value your talents: All you need to do is hang a sign on your door that shouts free whatever it is you're selling, and the line of new clients will extend into the next county.

FURTHER READING

ON MONEY

Money Is My Friend, by Phil Laut, is the best, clearest, most practical short course in money management: How to get it, invest it, and spend it. In short, how to become wealthy with a heart. Highly recommended.

Think, Set Goals, And Grow Rich, by Veronica Hurst. This marvelous book is the perfect sequel to **Money Is My Friend.**

For Love And Money, by Debra Kaplan, explores the connections, often constructive and destructive, among finances, romantic relationships, and the quest for power.

Grit, The Power of Passion and Perseverance, by Angela Duckworth. A bit simplistic for seasoned businesspersons, but an Ok start for students and persons entering the workforce.

ON WORK

The Power Of Dignity: The Thoughtful Leader's Model For Attracting And Keeping Stakeholders, By Pete Geissler. This book is *'A must-read for managers who want to reap the many fiscal and psychic rewards of dignity in business.'* John Larsen, President Emeritus, New Balance Athletic Shoe, Inc.; Director, NB (UK) Ltd.; and former president, World Federation of the Sporting Goods Industry (Lausanne).

Dignity examines, first, the very significant differences between managing for dignity and for stockholder value, then a number of successful businesses that are managed profitably and sustainably to protect and enhance the dignity of employees, customers, and other stakeholders, albeit in different ways and styles. The managers of those firms invariably ignore short-term accounting figures; they know that their businesses are much more than numbers and behave accordingly.

The Power Of Ethics: The Thoughtful Leader's Model For Sustainable Competitive Advantage, by Pete Geissler. *"This book proves that ethical behavior is the unstoppable power behind the happiness, prosperity, sustainability, and independence of individuals and firms. In fact, I will go further and say that it is the essential driver of every fulfilled life."* Jim Browne, founding partner, Allegheny Financial Group.

Ethics pays brief but pointed homage to theory and the great thinkers who have struggled for centuries to define ethics and its effects, then eschews those abstractions by leaping into practical usefulness by defining ethics—and its lack—by palpable behaviors and situations that readers can embrace or avoid. The special section on building an ethical organization in a hostile environment is applicable in equal doses to operations in less-developed and industrialized countries and in ethically immature organizations.

The Beanstalk Jackpots: Jack Hit Three Jackpots By Climbing His Beanstalk. You Can Too. By Pete Geissler

'If only, if only, if only I had met Pete Geissler years ago-I would have saved literally hundreds, maybe thousands, of hours working with toxic clients and employees and writing murky proposals and reports that lowered my productivity and profitability. Now I know better.' Susan Tusick, CEO, Tusick Architects Associates.

For almost fifty years since the early 1970s Pete Geissler wrote all sorts of marketing materials for all sorts of businesses and individuals, some of which were fairy tales. Pete thought that I was helping them deliver their many messages that would help them sell their products.

In truth, he was helping them to build better, more bountiful beanstalks, to help them hit their own personal jackpots.

Do What You Love, The Money Will Follow, by Marsha Sinetar. Her title/advice seems so perfect and universal that it is likely the most repeated aphorism at motivation conferences. Steve Jobs famously said that 'The only way to do great work is to love what you do.
If you haven't found it yet, keep looking. Don't settle.' Nevertheless, it isn't for everyone, and it's not a prerequisite for wealth and happiness. But I think it helps.

Peak by Chip Conley, a practitioner. PEAK posits that successful businesses rely on Abraham Maslov's hiearchy of needs to satisfy and enhance the loyalty of employees, customers, and investors, in turn raising profitability and sustainability.

Chained To The Desk, by Bryan Robinson, a screed on workaholics that I think confuses working long hours, i.e. workaholism, with a disease, alcoholism. Probably useless for entrepreneurs, whether beginning or seasoned, but possibly useful for their spouses and children.

Zen And The Art Of Motorcycle Maintenance, by Robert Pirsig, notes that *'This book offers another, more serious alternative to material success ...to something larger than just getting a good job and staying out of trouble...to a positive goal to work toward that does not confine.'*

ON COMMUNICATIONS AND THINKING

Critical And Creative Thinking, by Dr. Richard Paul and Dr. Linda Elder, the Foundation for Critical Thinking. The foundation's many booklets are designed to hone readers' creativity and imagination.. All are worthy of your attention and time.

On Writing, by Stephan King, a wildly entertaining and useful book from the master of suspense.

The Power Of Being Articulate: The Thoughtful Leader's Model For Wealth And Happiness, by Pete Geissler. *'The one basic skill needed in industry is the ability to organize and express ideas in writing and speaking.'* Peter Drucker, prolific writer of best-selling business books, Clark Professor of Social Science at Claremont Graduate School in California, and international management consultant. 1909-2005.

Throughout recorded history, many thinkers have noted the importance of being articulate and the power of words. This book, however, goes a giant step further by connecting articulation to wealth and happiness, and to the clear thinking and better decisions that thwart mediocrity. It quite correctly points out that we think in words, and we need more words to think with as the issues we need to resolve become more complex, as they do as we rise in any organization and as our close relationships mature.

The Power Of Writing Well: The Thoughtful Leader's Model for Business and Technical Communications, by Pete Geissler *'The tips in this accessible book can benefit every reader in important ways, regardless of discipline and experience.'* Charles Toran, President and CEO, Sci-Tek Consultants

Professional support: *"The most essential gift for a good writer is a built-in, shockproof shit detector."* Ernest Hemingway

"Editing yourself is your toughest job made easier if you follow one rule: delete everything that does not contribute to the story line, everything that does not further your purposes (s) or those of your receivers." Pete Geissler, from the book.

Writing better than your peers puts you in the lead for promotion or for success as an entrepreneur ... It also makes you a better speaker, your more public display of your intelligence. ..your only product.

Thinking Through Writing, by Susan Horton. I love this book and think of it as the perfect extension of **The Power Of Writing Well** since it transcends the rules of writing to the thinking and creativity that separates excellent from mediocre.

Writing To Learn, by William Zinsser, is a classic that was hailed by one critic as ' goes beyond the mechanics by explaining why writing is important.'

Success Built To Last, by Jerry Portas, Stewart Emery, and Mark Thompson, extends the concept of success to include a life of meaning, fulfillment, happiness, and lasting relationships. *'The question is why the rest of us tolerate any other definition,'*

The Rise Of The Creative Class, by Richard Florida, posits: *'Creativity has come to be valued—and new systems have evolved to encourage and harness it—because new technologies, new wealth, and all good economic things flow from it.'*

The Lessons Of History, by Will and Ariel Durant, especially Chapter IX, Socialism and History, which I have quoted several times in the text.

APPENDIX A. The Root Cause Of Success: Humility

Humble persons demonstrate awareness of the need to face and fairly address ideas, beliefs, or viewpoints toward which they are strongly opposed and/or have not seriously considered. They also demonstrate empathy toward and understanding of others by putting aside their own egocentricity. They avoid selective memory by thoughtfully considering and accepting, when appropriate, evidence from others that does not support their beliefs and decisions. They avoid oversimplification of complex issues and instead drill down by asking the why and how questions that discover a greater understanding of truth and morality. In short, they live with open minds and communicate openly and honestly.

A prominent sign of humility is interpersonal skills, or, as Daniel Goleman points out in his book, *Emotional Intelligence*, interpersonal intelligence, (it is) the ability to understand what motivates others and how they think and behave... the capacity to discern and respond appropriately to moods, temperaments, motivations, and desires.

Humility is demonstrated by willingness to change in constructive, sustainable ways.

APPENDIX B. The Root Cause of Failure: Arrogance

Arrogant people typically make unilateral decisions that they are absolutely certain are correct and beneficial largely for themselves and, at times, for others, yet those same decisions often create the opposite effects. But they don't care: They are so drunk with their egomania, power, and influence that negative consequences never enter their minds; either the consequences will never be discovered or the perpetrators delude themselves into thinking that they are above reproach or punishment of any kind.

Arrogant people and their destructions are endemic, and they share similar obnoxious traits. They're unaware of the limits of their knowledge; they are insensitive to surrounding circumstances and their own, and others', biases and points of view; are pretentious and boastful and show it by pretending to know more than they do; and they lack the logic needed to support their beliefs or decisions.

In short, they are so egocentric, so wrapped up in themselves that they easily, willingly, and foolishly believe that they are omniscient and protected from errors in any part of their current and future lives. They do not consider the consequences of their decisions and actions simply because they are certain that they are 'right' for themselves and, therefore, for everyone (their intellectual inferiors) who may be affected. They know what is best for others and impose that biased 'knowledge' on anyone willing to accept it.

Egocentrism is the root. Those afflicted with it judge the world from a narrow, self-serving perspective and typically are masters at self-deception and rationalization, maintain beliefs that are contrary to solid evidence, and violate ethical and moral standards while being perfectly confident in their righteousness.

While egocentrism and arrogance are endemic in business, perhaps it is even more so in sports. For example, Tiger Woods surely did not expect to be caught cheating on his wife, and when he was he lost many millions of dollars and the respect of millions of fans. Ben Roethlisberger, the Steelers' quarterback, followed the same path but, he says, is now a reformed family man. Pete Rose was caught gambling on the team he was managing, apparently not realizing the conflict of interest or, if he did, being convinced that his all-star status would shield him from any consequences. He was wrong.

All were displaying the traits or arrogant people:

1. Secrecy
2. Unwillingness or inability to listen to advice from others who often know more about the situation.
3. Unwillingness or inability to visualize or project the future consequences of current decisions.

APPENDIX C: Your Intelniche Is Your Brand and Your Competitive Supremacy

Intelligence, aka imagination or creativity, is your only product.

Businesspersons of all types—engineering, environmental, marketing, communications, writing, finance and so on—market nothing more than their individual or collective Intelligence. They display it or its lack by words and pictures, and it separates winners from losers.

We intuitively know intelligence when we experience it: the person who grasps and analyzes the situation at hand quickly and clearly communicates his or her understandings and conclusions; he or she demonstrates superior perceptions and verbal skills. Whether correctly or erroneously, we label those who don't, can't, or won't as not too bright, slow, and lacking credibility—exactly the labels that will destroy reputations and businesses in a heartbeat.

Intelligence has three components, all rare in business and society. Practicing all three creates, synergistically, the unique selling proposition—the intelligence niche, or, shortened, Inteliniche™—that wins contracts and sustains businesses:

1. Insight into the needs and wants of customers, created by active listening to understand. GIGO (Garbage In, Garbage Out) applies to the human mind as much as computers.

2. Creativity to convert insight into solutions that meet needs and wants most expeditiously and economically. Creativity was defined by Edwin Land, the inventor of instant photography, as the cessation of stupidity, or, on the other side of that coin, the perpetuation of intelligence.

3. Honesty to openly communicate accurately, clearly, and concisely. Knowledge is power is a useless and misleading aphorism if knowledge isn't communicated.

Your intelligence or its lack is displayed via blogs, websites, ads, papers, speeches, proposals, reports, letters, brochures, meetings and so on. Their overarching purpose is to paint themselves as more intelligent than competitors; nothing will enhance that purpose more quickly and thoroughly than clear, concise, on point English and design. Your communications—all of them—are the clearest and most enduring reflections of your intelligence.

The first step toward finding your Inteliniche is, again, insight, but this time it's listening to your most important client: yourself. Why did you win or lose a contract? Is there a pattern to your wins and losses? How can you transform a commodity—yes, intelligence is a commodity that cannot be monopolized—into your specialty.

The second step is, again, creativity, but this time it's the cessation of denial and the perpetuation of acceptance of why you win and lose, and then determining what you can do to win more often.

The third step is the honesty needed to examine all of your communications and reinforce those that specifically fit your findings of why you win and discard those that don't.

I advised a small engineering firm with a strong inteliniche in water management to forget the booming energy field—too many competitors who had already found their niches. They published a brochure that violates the language and is so generic that it offers not one reason to buy their services simply because there aren't any. The result after two years of marketing: zero contracts and big expenses.

My Inteliniche as a writer and teacher of writing focuses on engineers and scientists, and I eschew broadening my customer base simply because I lack the Inteliniche that I need for success.

The Moral: Operating within your Inteliniche enhances success; operating outside it enhances failure.

A potpourri of pitiful and perfect from the business of sports: Pittsburgh is a small city with three professional sports teams competing for entertainment dollars. The Pirates don't market quality because the team is a perennial loser, so they market, in ads, the vast number of games to fit anyone's schedule (time), special low-cost deals on tickets or food (price), and sideshows such as fireworks. Seats are always available. The team is profitable, but could be more so if it could market quality as well, as demonstrated by a surge in attendance during a rare winning streak. The Steelers and Penguins market quality: the teams are perennial contenders for championships and remind us of that often in ads and articles in newspapers. Neither markets price: tickets are scarce and costly, and there are no special deals. Nobody knows how profitable they are, but the best consensus is 'very'.

What's your Inteliniche? Are you exploiting it?

INDEX

A
adviser 8, 28, 30, 89, 91, 93
aphorisms 42, 48, 53, 75, 95
appreciate/appreciation 6, 25, 32, 40, 45, 46, 78, 93
arrogance 69, 82, 85, 125
articulate 1, 36, 39, 118
assets 13, 30, 37, 62, 90, 99, 100, 102, 112

B
Browne, Jim 78, 115

C
Carnegie Mellon University ... 4, 23, 27, 54, 64, 72
Churchill, Winston 108
collaboration 1, 42, 46, 48, 91
compartmentalize 66
Competitive Supremacy ... 1, 25, 127
conferences 12, 63, 116
conglomerate 7, 16, 21, 50, 69, 71, 72, 86
Conley, Chip 67, 117

connect/connections... 6, 25, 32, 36, 38, 112, 114
conscience 49
Cost leadership 26
Creative Breakthroughs .. 86
creativity 49, 62, 63, 65, 66, 68, 102, 117, 119, 127, 129
Critical Thinking 63, 68, 117

D
Darwin, Charles 66
Differential advantage 27
Divorce 1, 43
Dravo 15, 69
Drucker, Peter 2, 16, 18, 36, 67, 118
Duquesne University 4, 23, 24, 64, 72
Durant, Will & Ariel 108, 120

E
education 7, 61, 73, 78
Emerson, Ralph Waldo .. 39, 112
empathy/empathize 6,

32, 33, 37, 40, 45, 67, 93, 97, 101, 122
ENRON 15, 69, 83
ethics/ ethical 84, 115, 116, 125

F
Florida, Richard 120
Focus advantage 28
Ford Motor Company 30
Forster, E.M. 66
free enterprise 107, 109, 110, 111
freedom 19, 20, 46, 104, 111
Freud, Sigmund 107

G
Gates, Bill 61
generous/ generosity 13, 46, 76, 109, 111, 112
greed 28, 76, 80, 85

H
happiness 14, 16, 19, 36, 49, 65, 89, 96, 99, 103, 107, 109, 115, 117, 118, 119
health 50, 75, 99, 100, 101, 109, 113
Hemingway, Ernest 21, 119
Horton, Susan 87, 119
humility 78, 88, 122
Hurst, Veronica 114
Huxley, ... 2, 109

I
intelligence 7, 21, 62, 64, 65, 102, 119, 122, 127, 128, 129
intelliniche 12, 79
intrepreneur 8, 104

K
Kaplan, Deborah 114
King, Stephan .... See

L
leadership 34, 38
legacy 14, 23, 50

M
misstep
  employees 52
  restaurant 81
money 18, 20, 21, 38, 49, 56, 60, 61, 62, 76, 77, 78, 81, 82, 83, 92, 109, 112, 114

P
Picasso, Pablo 57
Pirsig, Robert 117
planning 81, 85
Portas, Jerry 119
publish/ publishing 24, 50, 54, 65, 74, 86
purpose 6, 18, 21, 24, 38, 43, 64, 66, 85, 112, 128

R
Rand, Ayn 67, 108
Robinson, Bryan 117

S
Seneca 81
Slevin, Dennis 36
soos 22, 23, 41, 71, 82, 83, 98, 107
Steve 49, 61, 116
success 8, 14, 16, 17, 24, 36, 37, 39, 61, 67, 89, 107, 111, 112, 117, 119, 129, 130

T
The Johnson O'Connor Research Institute 36
Tucker, Sophie 2

V
vacation 8, 96, 98, 99
value 26, 27, 28, 33, 44, 52, 54, 57, 63, 87, 93, 115

W
Wall Street Journal ... 37, 78
Wealth 21, 22, 23, 59, 103, 118
Westinghouse Electric Company 15, 42, 69, 70, 72

Y
Yasinsky, John 42

Z
Zinser, William 87

www.ingramcontent.com/pod-product-compliance
Lightning Source LLC
Chambersburg PA
CBHW030944240526
45463CB00016B/1784